Born to be Great

RANDALL J. BREWER

BORN TO BE GREAT

CONTENTS

VI –

INTRODUCTION

Every generation carries within it a divine thread - an unbroken line of men whom God Himself has called, shaped, and empowered to rise above the ordinary and walk in the greatness for which they were created. Greatness is not an accident of personality, talent, or circumstance. It is the intentional design of a purposeful God. From the dawn of time, the Father has placed His fingerprints upon those He calls, marking them for influence, significance, and impact on the earth. This book, "Born To Be Great," is built upon that eternal truth: every man of God was fashioned with greatness in mind, and so are you.

When we look through the pages of Scripture, we discover not stories of perfect men, but of chosen men - imperfect vessels with extraordinary destinies. Their greatness did not come from their natural ability but from God's supernatural calling. Abraham was a pagan idol-worshiper until God spoke his name and promised nations. Moses was a fugitive hiding on the backside of a desert until God lit a bush on fire and declared him the deliverer of Israel. Gideon was trembling in a winepress, convinced of his insignificance, until the Angel of the Lord called him a mighty man of valor. David, the overlooked shepherd boy, became Israel's greatest king. Peter, the impulsive fisherman, became the rock upon which Christ built His church. Paul, once a persecutor of believers, became the greatest apostle to ever carry the gospel to the nations.

What transformed these men into pillars of faith was not human ambition - it was divine purpose. God saw greatness in them long before they saw it in themselves. He spoke it, He confirmed it, and He cultivated it through seasons of preparation, struggle, testing, and victory. Their stories remind us that greatness is not something you grow into - it is something you were born with, planted into your very design by the Creator who formed you in your mother's womb.

Greatness, in the Kingdom of God, is not measured by worldly achievements, wealth, or fame. It is measured by obedience, surrender, and the courage to believe what God has spoken over your life. It is measured by the willingness to say, "Lord, here am I," even when circumstances appear impossible and the calling seems too heavy to carry. True greatness is found in walking out the assignments God has ordained for us from the beginning of time.

You were created with intention. You were crafted with purpose. You were called to make a difference, to influence your generation, and to carry out God's will on the earth. Whether you feel unqualified or unsure, whether you have failed or fallen short, the truth remains: you were born to be great. Not in your own strength, but through the power of the One who called you.

My prayer is that as you read this book, something awakens within you - an awareness of God's hand on your life, a stirring of vision, and a rekindling of passion to pursue the greatness He has destined for you. May the scriptures inspire you. May the promises of God anchor you. And may the Holy Spirit empower you to rise into the fullness of your calling.

The world is waiting. Heaven has spoken. And now, man of God, it is your time.

You were born to be great.

| 1 |

"DESTINED FOR GREATNESS"

Why were you born? If you are a true man of God, the answer is obvious. You were born to be great, to be a man destined to do great things on the earth. Yes, you were made for greatness. Settle it in your mind right now that God wants you to be great. In fact, He's disappointed if you don't want to be great. There is an assurance inside of you that you are great because God planned it to be so. It is therefore your responsibility to rise up and answer the call to be great. Every day you'll be given the opportunity to demonstrate focus, good judgment, maturity, integrity, character, compassion, honesty, self-awareness, discipline, and self-control. This is not the hour to shrink back, to doubt yourself, or to question what Heaven has already spoken over your life. Rise up with boldness and consistent confidence and become what God created you to be. You are a champion, and you've been called to be great in God's kingdom.

Men who are great are hungry for the opportunity to help make this world a better place. They're hungry for God to be glorified on the earth. Great men strive for peak efficiency in all they do. They go the extra mile in whatever endeavor they've taken upon themselves to accomplish. Each morning they wake up and seize the day. They start fast and finish strong. They run their race with a vision of victory forever on their mind. They are driven by a massive sense of urgency that the end is near and there is much work to be done before the Lord's return. The call to be great beckons you to embrace the moment. Now is the time to pursue your passion and aspiration to be great. You were not created to sit on the sidelines of your own life - you were created with purpose, with calling, and with gifts that the world needs. Every dream God placed inside you was planted with intention, and heaven is waiting for you to take the next step.

Wake up each morning knowing that greatness is your God-given destiny. You were born for greatness and there is no reason to settle for being average or mediocre. Ps. 18:35 (NLT) says, "You have given me Your shield of victory. Your right hand sustains me; Your help has made me great." The Passion Translation says, "You empower me for victory with your wraparound presence. Your power within makes me strong to subdue. By stooping down in gentleness, You make me great!" Eph. 2:10 says you were created as a masterpiece. God makes no mistakes and He is expecting you to live according to the good things He has planned for your life. You are God's workmanship programmed with a specific plan and purpose for your life. Your greatness is tied to God's vision of who you

are. He sees the potential within you that you may not yet recognize - the divine purpose that only He can fulfill. And He will
spare nothing for you to be great.

Greatness is a gift, but you must still earn it. You are not going
to be great just because it is God's will and then think you are
not meant to take any action. To be great you must persevere
on the journey to greatness and overcome obstacles. The journey to greatness is not smooth - it is shaped by challenges, detours, and obstacles that threaten to wear you down. But these
very tests are the tools God uses to refine, strengthen, and prepare you. You must strive to continue to do the things you
do with accuracy and focus. To be great you've got to be re-
lentlessly persistent. You'll let nothing stop you from accom-
plishing your goals for you understand that change is in your
hands. Embrace the call to be great. Answer the challenge and
let your determination guide you toward notable triumphs and
uncommon success. When you embrace the call to take action, you break free from hesitation and embrace the path of
progress. You press forward knowing that nothing can stop
you.

As a man of God, you are destined for greatness. Unfortunately, most men are running from their God-given destiny instead of running to it. Men of God are destined to be fruitful
and to walk in victory but fear, guilt, and deception has caused
them to miss the good things God has planned for their
life. This is why God wants to come into your life. He wants
to help you understand what your destiny is, to know who you
are in Him and what power and authority you've been given. A

part of the work God would have you do is help others see that they are also great. For that to happen, you must first know that you are great. One of the best kept secrets of success is having a positive opinion about yourself. Self-worth and high esteem are needed in order to become great. When you recognize your worth, you stop shrinking back, stop doubting your calling, and stop accepting less than what God has spoken over your life.

Self-worth comes when you know you've been created in the very image of God (Gen. 1:26,27). Ps. 139:14 says you are "fearfully and wonderfully made." Your worth is given to you by God. You are of great value to Him because of the price He paid to make you worthy, that price being the death of His Son on the cross. John 1:12 says God gave those who received Christ the right to become His children. When you see yourself as God sees you, you'll understand how much you're really worth. Your self-esteem, your sense of being a man of God, should not depend on what you say and do, but rather on who you are in Christ. Real men of God become great and attain self-worth and high esteem by having a right relationship with God and knowing how valuable they are to Him. A man who walks with God knows his worth. He recognizes that he is fearfully and wonderfully made, chosen, and beloved.

The most important thing you can learn after salvation is who you are in Christ. Why? Because when you know who you are, you'll know what to do. When you learn who you are, when you learn who God created you to be, you'll have more victories in your life for you have become great. You'll claim for yourself the life God wants you to live. Life will be more enjoyable because you're "the head and not the tail, above and not beneath" (Deut. 28:13). So who are you? Eph. 2:10 (AMP) says, "For we are His workmanship, His own master work, a work of art." The NLT says, "For we are God's masterpiece." In the hands of God you are being created to be great, to be models for human excellence and wellness, to be an ambassador for Christ on the earth (2 Cor. 5:20). You are being prepared to shine as a model of integrity, compassion, and strength - a living testimony of what it means to walk in God's ways.

Rom. 8:19 says, "For the creation waits with eager longing for the revealing of the sons of God." Yes, the whole world is groaning and waiting for you to reveal who you are. The problem with men today is they've lost their image of who they are. They've lost their identity, and they've lost their reason for living. Man was created in the image of God and to be a reflection of His glory. He was created to be a leader and a conqueror. He was created to be great. Real men are becoming an endangered species. Not because men are incapable of greatness, but because too many live for themselves rather than the purpose God created them for. True manhood is not measured by strength, success, or appearances - it is measured by character, integrity, faith, and the courage to lead, love, and serve as God intended. In a world where selfishness and instant gratification are celebrated, real men are rare, but they are needed more than ever.

To go from being average to being great you must stay connected to God, you must stay connected to people, and you must stay connected to yourself. Ps. 37:23 says, "The steps of a good man are ordered by the Lord." This is saying if you don't stay connected to God, you'll lose your identity as a man. Second, you must stay connected to people. You can't be great and help people if you're not connected to them. You can't reach the people you're called to reach. Third, you must stay connected to yourself. Many men are lost today because they don't know who they are, they don't know the person God created them to be. The world will tell a man to be consumed with getting fortune, fame, and power. Doing this will cause a man to lose perspective of who he really is. Mark 8:36 says, "For what will it profit a man if he gains the whole world, and loses his own soul?" Jesus is talking about temporary profit verses eternal loss.

To live only for earthly benefits is to waste your life. You can have all the world's goods at your disposal and in the end have nothing. For sure, death is the great equalizer. All these worldly pleasures will eventually fade away. You'll come to realize that you are nothing without God. Acts 17:28 says it's "in Him we live and move and have our being." God wants all men to acknowledge they are totally dependent upon Him for everything. When you realize that you'll seek no glory for yourself. The greatest idol in a man's life is his own glory. This is what brought about the fall of man in the Garden of Eden. Manhood is not easy so you can't lose sight of who God created you to be. If you lose sight of who you are, you'll lose sight of people and you'll lose sight of God. A man grounded in God's truth knows who he is and walks boldly in it. He understands that his identity is not defined by the opinions of the world, his successes, or his failures, but by the Creator who fearfully and wonderfully made him.

You were born to be great, to be a man of character, dignity, honor, courage, and strength. Strength, by definition, is having the capacity to do something. You need to realize that men were created to do three things. They were created to cultivate, created for conflict, and created to coach. The word "cultivate" means 'to improve or develop by careful attention, training, or study.' When you cultivate something, you work to make it better. Before you take any step in life, before you chase dreams, make decisions, or seek success, the most important work is the cultivation of your relationship with God. Like a tree planted by streams of water, your life will bear fruit only when rooted deeply in God's love. Greatness comes when you love, serve, and seek God with an undivided heart. Many men cultivate their physical bodies but not their inner man. They never pray, "Create in me a clean heart, O Lord, and renew a steadfast spirit within me" (Ps. 51:10).

A man's greatness is based on his relationship with God. Inside of most men is a dying young boy. He's got bulging muscles on the outside but is weak on the inside. Everything you build in life without God in it will crumble. No matter how strong the walls, how high the tower, or how impressive the achievements, if God is not at the center, it will crumble. Challenges will shake it, trials will test it, and without Him, it will fall. Most men today never cultivate their relationship with God. They've taken their hands off the plow. Jesus said, "No one, having put his hand to the plow, and looking back, is fit for the kingdom of God" (Luke 9:62). The MSG says, "You can't put God's kingdom off till tomorrow." Daily cultivate good habits such as prayer and meditation on scripture. Do acts of kindness to others and, most importantly, worship God and seek His will throughout the day. If you don't cultivate, you'll never be great. All you'll ever have in life is weeds that will choke out everything God wants to do in your life.

Cultivating good habits and character traits is essential for greatness because it helps you become more like Christ in your attitude, words, and actions. Jesus modeled for all of us what it looks like to cultivate healthy relationships. He spent a lot of time alone with the Father and demonstrated compassion wherever He went. Developing spiritual virtues such as love, joy, peace, patience, kindness, goodness, faithfulness, gentleness, and self-control (Gal. 5:22,23) are necessary for greatness to be achieved. If you'll walk in the fruit of the Spirit, you'll become great as you find deep fulfillment and purpose in life as you reflect God's love to others. You need to prepare your heart and mind for growth because it takes hard work to cultivate your spiritual life and become great. The seeds of faith grow into strength, wisdom, and fruitfulness not from comfort or ease but from intentional effort, daily discipline, and a willingness to be shaped by God's Word.

You will need to make time for prayer, meditation, and reflection on your beliefs. You'll need to seek out guidance from others who have traveled down the same path. Another key element to cultivate is a willingness to never quit when things are difficult and life seems uncertain, times when you're faced with challenges and doubts. You cultivate your relationship with God by actively seeking out His presence and making time for Him on a regular, daily basis. Strive to be like David who was described as a man after God's own heart. He spent his life seeking after God's will and building relationships with those around him. David spent time in prayer, worship, and reflection. Your heart is formed by the time you spend with God, allowing His voice to guide your decisions. David valued loyalty, compassion, and integrity. Let David's life inspire you to seek God earnestly, serve others faithfully, and strive to reflect His heart in all you do.

Man was created to deal with conflict, and he needs strength to do this. 1 Kings 2:2 says, "Be strong, therefore, and prove yourself a man." You are in a battle whether you like it or not. The great men of God prepare for battle by being mentally, physically, and spiritually ready. When the enemy comes, the prepared servant of God stands firm, unwavering, and victorious. They do not fear the fight because they have already been shaped by discipline, faith, and obedience. Life is hard and only the strong survive. You need to prepare yourself for battle. Declare each morning that you are victorious and no weapon formed against you will prosper (Is. 54:17). Joel 3:9 says, "Proclaim this among the nations, 'Prepare for war! Wake up the mighty men. Let all the men of war draw near. Let them come up." To be great you must wake up! 1 Peter 5:8 says to be alert and sober because your adversary the devil is roaming around like a lion seeking someone to devour.

To "wake up" is to embrace awareness of your gifts, your calling, and the ways you can serve others. It is a call to stop drifting in the ordinary and start living with extraordinary purpose. It's a spiritual alarm meant to stir your soul from complacency. Life is not meant to be lived half-asleep or on autopilot. It is a call to action, an invitation to rise with intention, a call for your life to be purposeful, a call to see the opportunities God has placed before you, and to step into the purpose He has uniquely designed for your life. Don't allow yourself to be weighed down in life by things that don't matter. You must get out of your comfort zone if you want to be victorious, if you want to rise up into a new level of thinking, a new level of believing, a new level of courage. Stop waiting for everything to be perfect and use what you already have. Each day you choose to wake up with mindfulness, gratitude, and determination, you align yourself with God's plan, fulfilling the mission He has set before you.

Man was also created to coach others into being great. They're to be role models and mentors. 1 Cor.11:1 says, "Imitate me, just as I also imitate Christ." The word "mentor" is defined as 'a wise and trusted counselor or teacher.' Coaching others to be great is a process dependent upon your submission to Christ. You lead by example. Charles Spurgeon said, "A Christian should be a striking likeness of Jesus Christ. We should be pictures of Christ." There is no better sermon than a good example. Words have power, but actions speak louder. People can hear sermons yet what often transforms hearts and minds is seeing faith in action. When you live a life of integrity and love you are preaching without uttering a single word. You coach others to be great by being the best imitator of Christ you can be, a pattern for others to follow. Coach others as God coaches you. Teach those who look up to you. Let your life be the sermon people can't ignore. Let your actions reflect the message your lips profess.

One of the greatest men in all the Bible was Abraham. Why did God choose him to be great? Gen. 18:19 (MSG), "Yes, I've settled on him as the one to train his children and future family to observe God's way of life, to live kindly and generously and fairly." Abraham was to coach others in the ways of the Lord. This meant he had to be careful, thoughtful, and attentive in conforming his actions with the ways of God. Being a mentor to others calls for a lifestyle of obedience. You can't coach others to be great if you're sinning all the time and are not great yourself. A mentor serves as a role model for others to follow. Phil. 4:9 (MSG) says, "Put into practice what you learned from me, what you heard and saw and realized." If mentors expect others to follow their example, they must be wholeheartedly committed to following Christ for this is what gives birth to greatness. Your influence is not measured by your words or titles, but by the authenticity of your devotion and the consistency of your faith.

| 2 |

"GREAT POTENTIAL"

God did not create you to live a moderate, low quality, mediocre life, a life where you do the same boring thing day after day after day. Men who live that way never do anything worthwhile with their lives. They go on living until one day they wake up and realize their life is almost over. The worst thing a man can do is live an average life, a life with no purpose and meaning, a life where no one will notice when he passes on to the other side. An average life is a life untouched by calling, unmoved by passion, and unaware of the divine assignment placed within the soul. It is a life where a man breathes but never truly lives, works but never truly builds, exists but never truly impacts eternity. Jesus made it very clear that you were born to be great. He said to the man who is born again, "The works that I do he will do, and greater works than these he will do" (John 14:12). God wants you to be great so you can do greater works than Jesus did, works that will bring glory and honor to Him.

When you understand your purpose, you'll begin to live out greatness in your life. Do that and you'll be more content and satisfied than you've ever been before. God has already arranged your path to greatness by preparing good works for you to do (Eph. 2:10). He wants you to be great so that greater works will come forth. You only become great when you understand your purpose clearly and begin to live it our fully. Be like Jesus who gave His life away wherever He went. Live a life marked not by self-interest, but by sacrificial love. Wherever you go, let your life echo His example. Let your words bring hope, your hands bring healing, and your heart reflect the boundless grace of God. Greatness must be lived out. It is revealed in the good things you do for other people, when you help make their lives better than it was before they met you. Greatness comes when you use your time, talents, and treasures to further God's kingdom on the earth with the right attitude where others see Christ in you.

You were born for greatness. Jesus never died to make you small, overlooked, or insignificant. He didn't go to the cross to diminish your value or to leave you in the shadows. On the contrary, His sacrifice was the ultimate declaration of your worth. He died to exalt you, to give you life in abundance, and to make you great - not by the standards of the world, but by the measure of heaven. When you became a follower of Jesus, greatness was placed within you. You are God's workmanship, a masterpiece of creation. Men who are successful believe in their own worth even when they have nothing but a dream to hang onto. Because of this, they're always ready to greet people with a smile. When meeting a stranger they always extend their hand first, looking the person in the eye when they do. This lets people know you're happy and confident being the person God created you to be. It's a way of showing people seeds of greatness are within you. You were born to be great because God wants you to be great.

No matter how small or mundane your obedience may seem, it is building greatness in you from the inside out. You were not born to live a defeated life. You were born to be extraordinary and to live beyond your circumstances rather than be defined by them. All men have God's promise that they can be great. However, to achieve greatness you will have to contend for it for there will be barriers standing in your way. Despite the fact that God had given the Promised land to the Israelites according to Josh. 1:1-3, they still had to fight to get possession of the land. The road to greatness is full of barriers. The road to greatness is never easy. Every path God sets before us is lined with obstacles meant not to stop us, but to strengthen us. These barriers test your faith, refine your character, and draw you closer to the One who called you. Each challenge is an opportunity to rely on His wisdom, seek His guidance, and walk in obedience.

Do not despise the barriers; embrace them for it is only through overcoming these trials that you arrive at true greatness. Barriers are not signs of failure; they are steppingstones toward the purpose He has prepared. They come because the enemy is trying to stop the greatness in you from coming forth. If you weren't a threat to him, he'd leave you alone. 1 Cor. 16:9 (TPT) says, "There's an amazing door of opportunity standing wide open for me to minister here, even though there are many who oppose and stand against me." Be encouraged knowing that opposition comes because wide doors are about to open for you, doors of favor and opportunity to take new ground. Many of the difficulties you face is because there is greatness inside of you. Like David, you are a giant-killer, a history-maker, and the devil doesn't like it. He knows who you are and who you're called to be. He sees the favor and anointing on your life. He sees that you are destined for greatness.

To stop your destiny from being fulfilled, there are five barriers he'll place across your path: damsels, distractions, disobedience, disappointments, and defeats. Men are tempted and distracted by women, money, and worldly opportunities. They get disconnected from the source of their strength and distractions set in. When men get distracted, they drift away from God, and their convictions begin to fade. This in turn leads to disobedience. The more you follow your plan instead of God's plan, you'll eventually be disappointed because nothing will turn out the way you thought it would. You'll be defeated in all you do. There is nothing more tragic than a man who has allowed defeat to take root in his heart. A defeated man is not simply weary; he is broken in spirit, lost in despair, and disconnected from the purpose God designed him for. It is from this place of inner defeat that anger, neglect, and irresponsibility often spring. It is a defeated man who abuses, abandons, and avoids their responsibilities.

Consider the life of Samson who was called to be a judge over Israel, to be a ruler and savior of God's people. He was a man called to do a powerful work. With great gifts and great intellect come great passions. Along came Delilah, a Philistine woman. Samson spent too much time with this damsel who was an enemy of Israel. Samson got distracted. He didn't manage his life well. He put his life and calling in the hands of Delilah. He disobeyed God and told her where his strength came from. Prov. 31:3 (NLT) says, "Do not waste your strength on women." The MSG says, "Don't spend your manliness on fortune-hunting, promiscuous women who shipwreck leaders." Manhood is a gift, a sacred energy entrusted to you by God, not meant to be squandered on fleeting pleasures or empty pursuits. The true measure of a man is not in the fortune he chases or the momentary allure of worldly temptations, but in the steadfastness with which he walks the path God has set before him.

Samson paid a heavy price for his disobedience. His hair was cut off, they bound him, gouged out his eyes, and put him at the grinding wheel in the prison. Sin takes away your greatness. It binds you, blinds you, and grinds away your relationship with God. Strength leaves when you are no longer repentant. Samson was distracted by a woman, by his own pride and arrogance. He was too easily entertained. He became self-confident instead of God-dependent. He lusted with his eyes and they were gouged out. There is nothing worse than a man without a vision. Prov. 29:18, "Where there is no vision, the people perish." How many men are walking around spiritually blind today? How many men are deceived thinking they're doing the right thing when in reality they're not? Samson was greatly disappointed in what he had done and was defeated when he died with the 3000 other Philistines. He died short of reaching his goal, of fulfilling his destiny.

God clothes men with greatness. It's like a cloak you get adorned with. It's a sign that you're destined to take new ground for the kingdom of God. With greatness you won't let any barrier or disappointment or injustice stop God's plan and purpose from being fulfilled in your life. With greatness comes resilience, and with resilience comes unwavering faith. No barrier, no disappointment, and no injustice can stand against the plan God has set for your life. High winds and tall waves didn't stop Jesus from getting to the other side of the lake. The mega storm didn't stop Him, and neither will it stop you. Why? Because you are great. You know that adversity is a sign that greatness is in you. Like Jesus you have the courage to stand up and boldly proclaim, "Peace, be still!" The difficulties you're facing are a sign something amazing is in your future. Your greatness is His instrument. This means your best days are ahead of you because nothing can stop what He has ordained.

God gives every man greatness and the ability to reach their full potential. He didn't create you to be average, He destined you to do great things with your life. God does not just see your potential - He sees your greatness. The greatness He places within you is not for self-glorification, but for the extension of His favor. When you embrace the gifts, talents, and character He has cultivated in you, you become more than yourself - you become a channel through which His blessings flow. Because you are blessed, you can be a blessing to others. You have great potential because within you lies a winner. You are destined for success and greatness, destined to leave a mark on this generation. Realizing this greatness will require you to unlock the potential God has placed inside you. This process involves a deep connection with your Creator. Go to Him and He'll reveal to you His will for your life. You must then take deliberate steps toward fulfilling that will. You must embrace the call of God on your life.

To overcome the barriers of life you must always prepare yourself for greatness. Preparation is when you become ready for what is desired. Adequate preparation will always receive glorious manifestations. 2 Chron. 27:6 says, "So Jotham became mighty, because he prepared his ways before the Lord his God." The MSG says, "Jotham's strength was rooted in his steady and determined life of obedience to God." In life, you don't get ready, you live ready. You become great by preparation. Talent is worthless without preparation. The future belongs to only those who prepare adequately. You prepare for greatness by staying focused, by fixing your eyes on the goal you intend to achieve. One of the greatest enemies of greatness is distraction. It whispers lies, diverts our attention, and tempts you to settle for less than what God has designed for you. Every moment you allow your focus to wander you delay the fulfillment of the purpose He has placed in your heart.

You must be persistent and have a bold determination to never give up. Matt. 24:13 says, "But he who endures to the end shall be saved." You must also prepare your heart for heart preparations determine earth manifestations. The soil of your spirit determines the fruit of your future. Before God manifests something on earth, He invites you to prepare a place for it within. Jer. 29:13, "And you shall seek Me and find Me when you search for Me with all your heart." To be great you must have faith in God that He is able to help you achieve greatness (Heb. 11:6). God is moved by faith so commit yourself to having unflinching faith in Him. To be great sacrifices have to be made. You must take up your cross daily and follow Christ (Luke 9:23). At the expense of earthly pleasures you must pay the price to obtain the prize. You must always be expectant. If you expect nothing, you will get nothing. Prov. 23:18 (NLT), "You will be rewarded for this; your hope will not be disappointed."

Dan. 11:32 says, "The people who know their God shall be strong and carry out great exploits." The NASB says they "will display strength and take action." This is a promise and a challenge wrapped in one. To "know God" is not merely to know about Him, but to have an intimate, personal relationship with Him - one that informs every thought, decision, and action. It is in this deep knowledge of God that true strength is found. Charles Spurgeon said, "To know God is the highest and best form of knowledge and this spiritual knowledge is a source of strength to the Christian." This is strength not measured by human might, but by spiritual resilience, courage, and unwavering faith. These great exploits are not ordinary achievements - they are divinely empowered acts that make a difference in the world. They may take the form of spiritual victories, acts of service, or breakthroughs in personal trials.

But the key is that these exploits flow from a deep connection to God, not from human effort alone.

God does not call His people to weakness or timidity. He calls us to stand firm, to rise above fear, doubt, and the challenges of life. Why? Because the strength we display is not merely our own - it is the reflection of His power at work within us. When you are strong, people recognize that He alone is the one true God. God wants it known that no barrier or obstacle is greater than His strength. This is why 2 Tim. 2:1 says to "be strong in the grace that is in Christ Jesus." When you know God in a personal way you will become great and do great things. You'll do illustrious acts and achievements, exploits that are rare and marvelous. Use your greatness to shine His light to a dark world and to spread His love to a hurting world. You are a winner, a champion, and you were created for success and greatness. Embrace this reality and be a vessel through which His power flows. Let His might shine brightly in every act of courage, every step of faith, and every word of hope you speak.

When you lean on Him, when you walk in faith and obedience, His strength becomes evident in your life. Mountains that once seemed insurmountable are moved, storms that once threatened to overwhelm you are calmed, and your heart that once trembled in fear finds courage. As Isaiah 40:29 reminds us, "He gives power to the weak and strength to the weary." When you accept His strength and walk boldly, the world sees not just you, but the glory of God reflected through your life. Let your life be a testament that God's strength is made perfect in your weakness. Be a vessel through which His power flows and let His might shine brightly in every act of courage, every step of faith, and every word of hope you speak. You're called to make a positive impact in the world around you. This is why you never settle for less when you're destined for more. Every true man should embrace the words of Eph. 1:11 (MSG), "It's in Christ that we find out who we are and what we are living for."

You will never discover how great you are by comparing yourself with others. You only discover your greatness through your relationship with Jesus Christ. In Christ you have great potential but potential by itself is not enough. To become great your potential has to give birth to purpose. The key to unlocking your potential and your greatness lies in your willingness to listen to God's voice and to act on His divine guidance. Be willing to step out of your comfort zone, to take risks in faith, to commit your plans to the Lord. As you do, the barriers to your success will fall away. You develop your relationship with Jesus so you can discover what He's put in you, those gifts and abilities that can help make the lives of other people better. Unlocking your potential is not merely about personal achievements, it's about utilizing your God-given gifts to serve others and to expand the kingdom of God on the earth. You have to discover what's in you so you can bring it out.

2 Tim. 1:6 (NLT) says, "This is why I remind you to fan into flames the spiritual gift God gave you." The term "fan into flames" is a verb and requires action on your part. Rise up and with great courage fan your gifts into a flaming fire. 2 Cor. 4:7 says, "But we have this treasure in jars of clay to show that this all-surpassing power is from God and not from us." There is

treasure inside of you and God put it there. This treasure is found in your unique qualities, talents, gifts, and abilities, plus the fire in your soul. Everything God placed in you has value and He uses it to bring glory to His name. Rekindle your fire so you can turn your potential into purpose and greatness. God put this treasure inside of you but it's your responsibility to get it out. Dig deep and find your fire, your passion, and your empowerment. Find your inspiration and determine to become all that God has destined you to be and do all that He has assigned your hands to do.

Ask yourself, "Who am I? Why did God put me here? How much potential do I have? How can I maximize my ability for His glory?" Within the answer to these questions lie the keys to greatness, the keys to unlock a fulfilling life, the keys that open the door to a bright future. Life is far too short to leave it incomplete and unfulfilled. Stop procrastination and fan the flame. Get to work doing what God has gifted you to do. Remember, greatness is more than potential, it's the execution of that potential. Zig Ziglar said, "When you catch a glimpse of your potential, that's when passion is born." Look past what you see on the outside and see there is so much more on the inside. Then decide to unleash your potential to the fullest. Live intentionally, not constrained by what the world sees, but empowered by what God has placed within you. Your inner life, your faith, your creativity, your courage are the treasures that will shape your destiny. Look within for the fullness of your potential is waiting for you.

| 3 |

"A TOUCH FROM GOD"

There are four things every man needs to be great that they can only get from Christ. They need acceptance, identity, security, and purpose. Every man carries within him a deep desire planted by God Himself - the desire to be accepted, valued, and understood. Not for what he pretends to be, not for the mask he wears to survive the pressures of life, but for who he truly is and what he stands for. The importance of this can't be overstated for out of acceptance flows positive self-worth and high self-esteem. The key is to not seek acceptance from people but from God. Eph. 1:6 says, "To the praise of the glory of His grace, by which He has made us accepted in the Beloved." We become great when we realize that we are accepted in God's sight. Oh, what a blessing it is to know that He takes delight in each and every one of us. Men become great when they discover their true identity, when they come to grips that they are a child of the King of kings and Lord of lords.

You are royalty. Eph. 2:19 says, "You are no longer foreigners and strangers, but fellow citizens with God's people and also members of His household." Your identity as a child of God gives you a sense of security. We know we are safe in His hands. Ps. 46:1 says, "God is our refuge and strength, an ever-present help in trouble." Every man needs a sense of purpose. Life just isn't worth living if we don't know why we're here. Purpose is the breath of the soul for without it even success feels hollow. But with it, even battles become worthwhile. The key is to follow God's purpose for your life and not your own. Greatness comes when you accept the fact that you were "created in Christ Jesus for good works" (Eph. 2:10). Serving God and being good to people is what you were created to do. God has created us as new creatures so that we might walk with Him and bear good fruit that remains (John 15:5). You become great when you help make the lives of other people better.

Jesus said in Mark 10:42 that the world wants to show you its greatness. When it comes to the kingdom of God, the Heavenly Father has a different standard of what makes you great. Mark 10:43 says, "Yet it shall not be so among you; but whoever desires to become great among you shall be your servant." Vs. 45, "For even the Son of Man did not come to be served, but to serve, and to give His life a ransom for many." In the kingdom of God greatness is service, not status. Greatness is based on what we do for others without drawing attention to ourselves. The Bible teaches us quite clearly that it is impossible to love Jesus without serving people. To be great, to have a life that matters, you must do good to other people. John 13:1

says Jesus loved His disciples to the end and then He washed their feet. He showed His love to the very end because there is no end to His love. Don't criticize those with dirty feet. Instead, be great and wash their feet.

When Jesus knelt to wash His disciples' feet, He wasn't performing a simple act of cleanliness - He was revealing the very heart of God. The King of the universe wrapped Himself in a towel, stooped low, and served those who would soon betray, deny, and abandon Him. And then He said, "If I washed your feet, you also ought to wash one another's feet." True greatness in God's kingdom isn't measured by titles, achievements, or applause. It's measured by how willing we are to take the lowest place for the sake of love. Follow the leading of the Lord and you'll become great. Isaac obeyed God and Gen. 26:13 says, "And the man became great, and went forward, and grew until he became very great." Yield to the Spirit of God for He alone has the blueprint for your greatness and success. Refuse to go in a direction that is contrary to what God has called you to do. Greatness is your heritage. Always have the consciousness that you're destined for greatness. All it takes is a willingness to be the servant of all.

Never forget who you are and why you were born. Eph. 2:10 (AMP) says, "For we are His workmanship, His own master work, a work of art." You were "created in Christ Jesus, reborn from above, spiritually transformed, renewed, ready to be used for good works which God prepared for us beforehand." Prov. 18:16 says, "A man's gift makes room for him and brings him before great men." God has placed something unique inside every person. You were not born empty. You were born gifted, carrying a divine deposit that Heaven intends to use to bless the world. Your gift may appear ordinary to you, but in God's hands it becomes a key that unlocks doors no human could force open. God uses the gift He placed within you to shape your destiny. When you cultivate what God has given you - your compassion, your ability to teach, your wisdom, your creativity, your leadership, your generosity - He causes that gift to create opportunities that allow you to be a blessing to those around you.

Use the talents God gives you and you'll be given access to important people. God has put a gift or talent in every man and promises that the world will make room for it. It is this gift that will enable you to walk in your divine calling. Every man's gift is a God-designed blend of spiritual capabilities which acts as a channel through which the Spirit of God ministers to others. What you were designed to be known for is your gift. It is in exercising this gift that you will find real fulfillment, purpose, and contentment in the work you do. God created you to expand His kingdom on the earth. No matter how big the world is, there's a place for you in it when you discover and manifest your gift. God has enabled you to reach people that no one else can, and it is the giftings He has graciously given you that will open doors of opportunity for you. Rom. 12:6 says, "Having then gifts differing according to the grace that is given to us, let us use them." The MSG says, "Let's just go ahead and be what we were made to be."

We all have different gifts according to the specific gift of grace that is given to us. Before you spoke your first word or took your first step, God had a plan and purpose for your life. Your purpose is found in God and He will not allow you to lose it. Discover what's in you so you can be great and soar like an eagle, so you can run and not be weary, so you can walk and not faint (Is. 40:31). A spiritual gift is an ability God has given you. It enables you to do something so naturally and smoothly that others will ask you to do it and enjoy watching you do it. A spiritual gift is a fulfilling thing when you are using it. It is not a hard, painful thing to do. Instead, it is something you take great delight in doing. The more you use your gift, the bigger it gets. It is like a well-toned muscle that gets stronger and more powerful each time it is tested. Over time as you become excellent in your gift, it gets noticed by others and, as you prove yourself trustworthy, God will open doors for you that you could never imagine.

David had the gift of courage, leadership, and the ability to accurately swing a slingshot. These gifts opened the door to his future as the king of Israel. Joseph was a slave and prisoner but had the gift to interpret dreams. That gift brought him before Pharaoh who put Joseph in charge of the entire nation of Egypt. Moses only had a staff in his hand, but God used it to part the Red Sea. A young boy only had five loaves and two fish, but God used them to feed thousands. Whatever your gifts and talents may be, God wants to use them. Prov. 22:29, "Do you see a man skilled in his work? He will stand before kings." The MSG says, "Observe people who are good at their work. Skilled workers are always in demand and admired.

They don't take a backseat to anyone." You were not created without purpose. The abilities you carry - whether they seem great or small - were placed in you by the very hands of God. When you develop the gifts God has given you, He positions you in places you never imagined.

We are not citizens of this world - we are travelers passing through, pilgrims on a journey toward a heavenly home. Scripture reminds us that "our citizenship is in heaven" (Phil. 3:20), and that everything we see here is temporary. Yet God, in His wisdom, has placed us on this earth for a purpose. While we walk this temporary path, we have been entrusted with something eternal: the gifts, talents, and callings God has placed within us. These are not meant to be buried, ignored, or wasted. They are the tools God gives us so that, even as strangers in this world, we can make a lasting impact on it. So while we are here - however long this journey lasts - let's choose to leave this world better than we found it. Let's love deeply, serve faithfully, encourage boldly, and shine the light of Christ in the dark places we pass through. Let's build up, not tear down; heal, not hurt; offer hope, not despair. For though this world is not our final home, it is our current mission field.

God can and will use anybody. He used Gideon to deliver Israel from the Midianites but before that he was nothing more than a cowardly farmer. Jephthah was the son of a prostitute, but God used him to deliver Israel from the Ammonites. Ruth was a pagan, yet it was through her genealogy that Jesus was born. God wants to use you so start where you are and keep moving forward. David was but a lad when he defeated Goliath and later became king over all Israel. Don't allow anyone to limit you because of your age. Joash was king at age seven (2 Chron. 24:1) and Abraham was a hundred years old when Isaac was born (Gen. 21:5). 1 Tim. 4:12 (NLT), "Don't let anyone think less of you because you are young. Be an example to all believers in what you say, in the way you live, in your love, your faith, and your purity." Ps. 92:14 says, "They shall still bear fruit in old age; They shall be fresh and flourishing." Be like Aaron who served God until he turned 123 years of age.

Greatness begins when you take your everyday ordinary life and surrender it to God. No matter what your lot in life has been, great men never allow where they've been and how they started to dictate and determine where and how they finish. God said in Is. 43:18,19 (MSG), "Forget about what's happened; don't keep going over old history. I'm about to do something brand new. it's bursting out! Don't you see it?" Consider Esther who was a slave before God used her to save her people from being massacred. Like Esther, you are here on purpose, for a purpose (Esther 4:14). Who did God chose to be the mother of Jesus? A famous actress? A great athlete? A celebrity? No, He used a humble peasant girl named Mary. Greatness is always attached to the willingness to be used by God. Mary told the angel Gabriel, "Let it be done to me according to what you have said" (Luke 1:38). Don't wait until you feel qualified. God is calling you now. All He asks is that you make yourself available.

In a world that measures worth by accomplishments, titles, and the size of our achievements, it's easy to believe that God is waiting for us to "become something" before He can use us. But God has never been impressed by human greatness - He is moved by a willing heart. When Isaiah stood before the Lord, he wasn't standing in a place of strength or perfection. He had just confessed, "I am a man of unclean lips," overwhelmed by God's holiness and his own inadequacy. Yet in that sacred moment, something powerful happened. God touched him, cleansed him, and prepared him for divine purpose. Then came the question that still echoes through the ages, "Whom shall I send, and who will go for Us?" God wasn't looking for the most talented, the most educated, or the most confident. He was looking for someone willing. Someone available. Someone whose heart was ready to say yes even before knowing the assignment. Isaiah responded with one simple, life-changing declaration, "Here I am. Send me!"

Never doubt whether or not God can use you. Remember that Jacob was a master of deception, Solomon was an unusual lover, Elijah was suicidal, and Noah was drunk. Remember also that Abraham was old, Jeremiah was young, Isaiah preached naked, Leah was not beautiful, Samson was a womanizer, and Rahab was a prostitute. Gideon doubted his own worth, David was an adulterer and murderer, the disciples fell asleep when Jesus needed them most, and the Samaritan woman had too many men in her life. Matthew was a tax collector and was hated and despised by all men. Still, God used him to write one of the four gospels. Many of the disciples were just common fishermen who would go on to turn their world upside down. Paul persecuted the church and went on to write most of the New Testament. All these people had many flaws, but God still used each of them greatly and He can and will use you. Yes, even little ole you. Just remember how great you are.

You are great because God is on your side. He is with you and in you. You've been redeemed and have received the Spirit of adoption (Rom. 8:15). You are great because you have dominion over guilt and shame. Rom. 8:1 says there is no condemnation, no guilt, and no shame to those who are in Christ Jesus. You are great because you have dominion over defeat and the devil. 2 Cor. 2:14 says, "Now thanks be to God who always leads us in triumph in Christ." The ESV says, "But thanks be to God, who in Christ always leads us in triumph procession, and through us spreads the fragrance of the knowledge of Him everywhere." 1 John 4:4 speaks about men who are great, "You are of God, little children, and have overcome them, because He who is in you is greater than he who is in the world." You are great because of "the utter extravagance of His work in us who trust Him - endless energy, boundless strength!" (Eph. 1:19 MSG).

To be great, you have to always remember who you are and why you're here. Somebody out there needs you so definitely you "were born for such a time as this" (Esther 4:14). To save her people from annihilation, Esther put her own life at risk. She was reluctant at first but trusted God to help her do what needed to be done. Like Esther, you may face uncertainty, failure, fear, and suffering as you try to fulfill God's plan for your life. The good news is God is with you every step of the way. Just know that you are where you are for a reason so don't complain and try to get out of your call. Dig your heels in and march into battle. Many times, being chosen by God comes with an assignment you don't want to be called to. Jonah ran from his call to preach at Nineveh and look what happened to him. Men who are great don't run from their call even when fulfilling it will bring misery and discomfort. No, real men run to the sting of battle. Don't focus on the pain but be grateful that God is using you in such a time as this.

Stand strong and be great knowing that there will be times God won't rescue you in the storm because He wants to use you as a lifeboat for someone else. Men who are great are anchored in Christ thus they are not tossed to and fro. Ps. 91:13 (MSG), "You'll walk unharmed among lions and snakes, and kick young lions and serpents from the path." You have to grow and mature into a place of greatness that is willing to do whatever God tells you to do even if there is a great price to pay to do it. Jesus prayed to the Father, "Father, if You are willing, please take away this cup of horror from Me. But I want Your will, not Mine" (Luke 22:42 NTB). Great men trust God enough to continue to pursue His purpose for their lives even when they keep running into problem after problem after problem. Without a doubt, fulfilling God's call is not for the weak and cowardly. On the contrary. It will be by far the hardest thing you'll ever have to do in your life, so you have to be strong and courageous.

You have to trust God enough to continue to follow His plan and stay on track even when life tries to derail you every step of the way. Esther realized she had been made queen to save lives. Even with the possibility of being put to death, she risked her life to rescue her people from harm. Likewise, God has placed you where you are to save lives. He has put people within your reach and influence so you can rescue them from the grasp of the enemy. Never let a moment of misery cause you to lose sight of why you're here. Your purpose in life is to encourage people and help them find restoration and redemption. Your assignment is to bring life to a dying world, and you can't afford to let distractions get in your way. You can't let people suffer because you're too consumed with your own hurt. Yes, your pain is real, but it cannot become your prison. When you become so wrapped in your own wounds that we stop seeing the wounds of others, you miss the very heart of Christ.

There is no time to wallow in self-pity when so many people are wounded and need a touch from God. Your pain is irrelevant when you've got a destiny to fulfill. You are here to give hurting people a glimpse of God in their pain. God needs you to be His mouth, His hands, His feet, and His comforting and encouraging presence in this world. You are here to tell people that God is able to give them the help they need. Say to them, "In all these things we are more than conquerors through Him who loved us" (Rom. 8:37). Your words, actions, and attitude show people how to go through the valley they are in and never give up. Show them your greatness and they'll follow your lead. People are watching you and listening to you. Don't do harm to the image and likeness of God that you are by living in a mansion of misery all the time. Take a stand and be great. Do something that will better the lives of others. Work diligently knowing that the last hours are upon us.

| 4 |

"STAND YOUR GROUND"

Every person alive is born for a certain purpose. Jesus was born to be a Savior, David was born to be a king, you were born to be great. Greatness is in you so rise up to its call. God has placed within you a divine spark, a unique purpose meant to shine in the world. Every gift, every talent, every dream is a seed of greatness that He has entrusted to you. The calling may seem daunting, the path uncertain, but know this: the power to rise, to overcome, and to fulfill your purpose already dwells within you. Don't let the giant of greatness in you sleep because of your situation and circumstances. Do not shrink back in fear or doubt. Step forward in faith, embrace the potential God has placed inside you, and walk boldly into the life He has prepared. Fan the flame of your passion. Renew your commitment to the vision God placed in you. Your greatness is not measured by the applause of others, but by the courage to rise, the obedience to your calling, and the love and light you bring to those around you.

Accept the picture of the true essence of your creation. Don't let the world put limits on you and on what you can achieve. You have inside of you what it takes to scale walls and leap over mountains. There is no force in the world that can stop you once you make the commitment to keep going forward and to climb higher and higher. Never accept mediocrity in your life. Rise and shine for you are a product of excellence and greatness is in you. You are a warrior, and greatness will take you to the top of the mountain. Break the barriers and push back those things that try to hold you back. Rise up knowing that all things work together for your good (Rom. 8:28). Your light is shining bright, and people everywhere will come to the radiance of your rising. You are great so believe in your ability to meet any challenge. Your works of greatness will provoke others to seek your hand for great feats. Go forth and excel. God has designed you for greatness, for elevation, for promotion, for dominion, and for success.

Great men don't run away when obstacles rise before them. When barriers appear, they don't cower in fear or shrink back in doubt. No, their faith is greater than their fear. They understand that challenges are not meant to break them, but to build them. They stand firm, grounded in purpose and anchored by God's strength. They press forward when others turn back, fight when others surrender, and shine as examples of perseverance. True greatness is not measured by comfort or ease, but by the courage to keep standing, to keep fighting, and to keep trusting in God's plan, no matter the storm. They're like Eleazar who by himself "stood his ground and fought the Philistines until his hand was weary and stuck to his sword" (2

Sam. 23:10). Eleazar was one of David's three mighty men and, because he stood his ground, "the Lord accomplished a great victory." In battle, who you are on the inside shows up and reveals its true colors. Eleazar's comrades ran away that day and revealed they were not great.

Men who are great don't run away; they don't try to get out of anything prematurely. They stay and fight and become mature, well-developed men of God. Progression is our ultimate goal and great men keep going forward no matter what. Sad to say, most men give up far too quickly and far too often. Great men don't run from fear, they run to it knowing God has not given them a spirit of fear but of power, love, and a sound mind (2 Tim. 1:7). The Amplified Bible says, "God did not give us a spirit of timidity, of cowardice, of craven and cringing and fawning fear." The word "cowardice" can be defined as 'a failure of spirit caused by fear.' Being fearful involves a moral deficiency for it reveals a lack of faith. Instead, "He has given us a spirit of power and of love and of calm and well-balanced mind and discipline and self-control." God gives great men power and aggressive energy in the face of difficulty which overcomes the weakness of fear, doubt, and cowardice.

Stand strong when the winds of adversity blow fiercely against you and never let your flame die down when confronted with the prospects of suffering. Is. 12:2 says, "God is my salvation, I will trust and not be afraid." Let your faith be the anchor that holds you firm when uncertainty threatens to shake you. Your flame - the light of hope, love, and trust in God - must never be allowed to flicker out. Remember, the fire within you is fueled not by circumstances but by the Spirit of God who dwells in you. Suffering may come, but it cannot defeat the steadfast heart that trusts in the Lord. Every trial is an opportunity to grow stronger, shine brighter, and reflect the glory of God more fully. Hold fast to His promises, lift your eyes above the storm, and keep your flame alive. For the one who endures with faith will emerge not only victorious but as a beacon for others walking through their own darkness. Suffering may come, but it cannot defeat the steadfast heart that trusts in the Lord. Stand firm and let your light never fade.

Eleazar kept fighting even though he was weary, exhausted, and tired. Yet, despite all this, he never let go of his sword. His persistence, determination, and perseverance saved the lives of many people that day. A great victory took place all because one man stood his ground. For sure, he did not have the spirit of timidity. He was a great man, a fearless warrior who faithfully fought on even when the odds were against him. Great men continue to serve the Lord with all their strength in spite of opposition. They say, "In God I have put my trust; I will not be afraid. What can man to do me?" (Ps. 56:11). Jesus said in John 14:27, "Let not your heart be troubled, neither let it be afraid." Great men say, "If God be for us, who can be against us?" (Rom. 8:31). British missionary Hudson Taylor said, "All God's giants have been weak men who did great things for God because they reckoned on His being with them." Great men are "strengthened with power through His Spirit in the inner man" (Eph. 3:16).

The Message Bible says this is "not a brute strength but a glorious inner strength." We receive power to live a supernatural life. Micah 3:8 says, "But truly I am full of power by the Spirit of the Lord, and of justice and might." David said in Ps. 23:4, "Yea, though I walk through the valley of the shadow of death, I will fear no evil for You are with me." A valley is not a bad place to be if you know God is there with you. Great men know He's not the light at the end of the tunnel; He's the light in the tunnel. Great miracles take place in the midst of grave circumstances. Think about it. Where of all places did God prove His faithfulness to Daniel? In the lion's den! Likewise, where did God reveal Himself to the three Hebrew children? In a fiery furnace that was heated seven times over! Notice that God did not take these men out of their difficulty. But He was there beside them, walking hand-in-hand with them every step of the way. He was the light in their tunnel of chaos and despair.

Great men serve God with gladness knowing He'll never leave them or forsake them (Heb. 13:5). They won't be stopped by hungry lions or a burning furnace. What should you do in a valley? Keep walking. David walked through the valley he was in not stopping along the way to succumb to worry and doubt. No, he trusted God and great men do the same. Like Paul, they "press on toward the goal for the prize of the upward call of God in Christ Jesus" (Phil. 3:14). When you believe God is with you, the depth of your faith will propel you to do great exploits in His name despite what is coming against you. Continue to trust God no matter what you're going through knowing that when all is said and done, you'll be standing victorious with arms held high giving praise to your Lord and Master. No matter the storms or the valleys you walk through, continue to trust in the Lord. Hold fast to His promises, for He is faithful and true. Every struggle, every challenge, is shaping you for the victory He has prepared.

Keep your eyes on Him, and when the battles are over, you will stand triumphant with arms lifted high, heart overflowing with praise, declaring the glory of your Lord and Master. Remember, the God who holds the universe also holds you, and in Him, you are more than a conqueror. It is no secret that life is not fair or easy, and all men get knocked down from time to time. It's the great ones who wipe the dust off themselves and get back up. Micah 7:8 says, "Do not rejoice over me, my enemy. When I fall, I will arise. When I sit in darkness, the Lord will be a light to me." The enemy gloats and gets great satisfaction at the misfortune of God's people. They celebrated the death of Jesus not knowing what would happen three days later. Men who are great are confident of their eventual triumph. When they do fall, either openly or secretly, they arise before the enemy gets time to rejoice. Real men stir up greatness from within. They get on their feet a relentless determination to march back into battle.

When knocked down, real men rise with relentless determination refusing to remain in the shadows of defeat. Every setback becomes fuel, every challenge a call to action. They march back into battle with courage anchored in faith, knowing that strength is not measured by comfort, but by perseverance. Charles Spurgeon said, "There is sure hope for us in the Lord. If we are trusting in Him and holding fast our integrity, our season of down casting and darkness will soon be over. The insults of the foe are only for a moment. The Lord will soon turn their laughter into lamentation and our sighing into singing. Let us take heart, for we shall overcome him before long. We shall arise from our fall, for our God has not fallen and He will lift us up. We shall not abide in darkness, although for a moment we sit in it. Our Lord is the fountain of light, and He will soon bring us a joyful day. Let us not despair or even doubt. Woe unto those who laugh now, for they shall mourn and weep when their boasting is turned into everlasting contempt."

True greatness is born in the willingness to stand, to fight, and to honor the purpose God has placed within them. In order to be great, you must be willing to be different from everybody else. And to be different, you must be willing to be a person who takes risks. Taking a risk means there is the possibility that something unpleasant will happen. However, greatness and anything else worth having is worth the risk. You can't obtain what you don't go after so press forward no matter what. Take the risk and do something new and different. Taking a risk to become great is a worthwhile endeavor. For sure, it's worth the risk to get all God has for you and to become all that He has called you to be. There is a poster showing two mountain climbers straining to reach the top. The inscription said, "Conquest without risk is a triumph without glory." The level of your greatness is based on the risks you are willing to take. Just know that low risk brings low return and high risk brings high return.

God had given the people of Israel the Promised Land but they allowed taking a risk to stop them from possessing what God had given them. God's promises are not for the faint of heart - they are for the bold, the faithful, and the obedient. Your personal Promised Land - the place of blessing, purpose, and fulfillment that God has prepared for you - cannot be entered by playing it safe. It requires courage, faith, and a willingness to step into the unknown. The journey begins with trust - trust in God's integrity, His timing, and His provision. When you fully believe that He is faithful, you are empowered to take risks that others shy away from leaving behind comfort zones, confronting fears, and embracing the challenges that stretch your faith. Remember, those who did cross over did not enter Canaan from the sidelines. They crossed the Jordan, faced giants, and claimed the land that God had promised. Their success wasn't because the obstacles were small, but because their God was mighty and trustworthy.

Possessing your own personal Promised Land all depends on whether or not you trust the integrity of God enough to take big risks. Num. 23:19 says, "God is not a man that He should lie. Has He said, and will He not do it? Or has He spoken, and will He not make it good?" God never makes promises He won't keep. He always keeps His word. He fulfills it and makes it come true. If He said the Promised Land is yours, it's yours! Your Promised Land awaits, but it cannot be possessed without faith-driven action. Trust God enough to take the steps He calls you to - even the big, uncomfortable, faith-stretching steps. Your obedience opens the door to His blessings, and your faith transforms uncertainty into triumph. When you choose obedience, you align your life with God's perfect will. Each act of faithfulness, no matter how small, opens the door to His abundant blessings. Obedience is not a burden - it is the key that unlocks the treasures of heaven.

Faith, on the other hand, transforms the shadows of uncertainty into the light of triumph. Even when the path seems unclear, trusting God turns obstacles into opportunities and trials into testimonies. Your steps of obedience, guided by unwavering faith, become the pathway to victory. The Promised Land was inhabited by giants, and whether the people could experience all that God had prepared for them depended on their willingness to trust Him enough to take bold risks. Twelve spies had explored the land of Canaan and reported back on the fabulous beauty and bounty they found there. It was truly a land flowing with milk and honey. However, ten of the spies chose to focus on the risks of taking the land while Joshua and Caleb focused on God who had promised them the land. The ten spies focused on the giants who lived there but Caleb boldly declared, "Let us go up at once and possess it for we are well able to conquer it" (Num. 13:30).

The ten spies were not great; Joshua and Caleb were. Why? Because they believed God who said they could take the land. When God gives a promise, there is nothing to worry about. Nothing can stop what God starts. Phil. 1:6 (GWT), "I'm convinced that God, who began this good work in you, will carry it through to completion on the day of Jesus Christ." If you're going to possess what God has for you, it will take some risk. You will reap a reward if you're convinced that what God promised you will come to pass. The word "convince" means 'to cause to believe firmly in the truth of something; to persuade to do something.' In Latin it means 'to overcome; to conquer.' The people who followed the lead of the ten spies who said the risks were too great never entered the Promised Land. Eventually they all died in the wilderness. Be careful who you trust, who you share your hopes and dreams with. When you're ready to take a big risk, be careful of those who will try to discourage you.

When you get ready to obey God and fulfill your destiny, be prepared to take some risks. The greatest barrier of all is not obeying God because you won't risk it all. For sure, you'll miss the top of the mountain if you listen to every molehill doubter along the way. You'll miss the best God has for you. You'll miss the Promised Land. The mountain is before you so start climbing. You'll never see the view from the top if you don't take a risk and stay where you've always been. It's time to get started before you miss out on God's best. It's time to dream big, to broaden your vision, to enlarge your territory, to go further, to reach higher. Christopher Columbus said, "You can never cross the ocean unless you have the courage to lose sight of the shore." Many lives have been wasted because people weren't willing to take a risk. The truth is, one of the greatest risks in life is never daring to take a risk. Yes, a ship is safe in the harbor but staying there is not what ships are for.

If you're not willing to take a risk then all you'll do is live an ordinary, mediocre life. There are no great accomplishments without risk. Poet T. S. Eliot said, "Only those who will risk going too far can possibly find out how far one can go." Greatness begins at the end of your comfort zone, when you're willing to take a risk and get out of the boat and with daring faith step out onto the water. It is better to take a risk and become great than to be like those who live in a gray twilight and know nothing about what the life of a warrior is all about. All men should have the desire to be great, to be significant, to have their lives matter. In fact, all men are hardwired for greatness. Never forget that you were created in the image of a great God. You are God's workmanship, a masterpiece, and there is greatness inside of you. God has put certain gifts and talents and abilities inside of you that He wants you to cultivate and use for the purpose of doing great things for His glory.

It is not wrong to want to be great. It is God who put that desire inside of you. He wants you to be great because He is great. There are things inside of you that you can't even see right now but God will pull them out of you because He created you for a purpose. Gideon had a low opinion of himself and didn't see anything good inside of him. Then one day God came to him and said, "You're a mighty warrior, a man of valor." God is not honored if all you do is strive for mediocrity, to be normal, to go with the flow, to say, "Whatever happens, happens. Whatever will be, will be." No, God is honored when those men who are made in His image pursue greatness, pursue destiny, and pursue purpose at all costs. You are wired for greatness with the purpose of making a positive difference in the world. There is greatness inside of you and God wants you to do great things with it. Walk around with the confidence that God can and will use you in an incredible way, that He will do great things in you and through you.

| 5 |

"THE EYES OF GOD"

To be great you must see yourself through the eyes of God. You can't get stuck on the way you are now but must instead focus on who and what you can become. Great men do not become mighty warriors for God by accident. They rise because they see something within themselves that others often overlook. When they look in the mirror, they don't just see who they are - they see who they can become through the power of God working in them. Great men recognize their God-given potential. They sense abilities within them that may still be undeveloped, small, or hidden, but they know these seeds can grow into strength, influence, and spiritual authority. They understand that the gifts God placed inside them are not there to be buried - they are meant to be cultivated. A warrior is not born fully skilled; he is shaped. He becomes mighty by allowing God to sharpen his courage, deepen his character, and train his hands for battle. Great men welcome that process.

Instead of shrinking back, they embrace discipline, growth, and the stretching seasons that prepare them for future success and usefulness. They refuse to let past failures or present limitations define them. Instead, they cling to God's vision for their lives. They remain steadfast and keep their hearts fixed on the plan God has given them. Where others see weakness, God sees a warrior in training. And great men choose to believe God's report over their own doubts. Every mighty warrior in Scripture began as someone ordinary - but God saw more. And they chose to agree with Him. God is still calling men to rise up, to develop what He has placed within them, and to step boldly into the future He has prepared. Those who respond - who see their potential and surrender it to God - become vessels of power, purpose, and divine impact. Great men become mighty warriors when they believe that God can make them more than they are and they let Him do the shaping.

In Judges 6:15 Gideon saw his family as the least significant in Manasseh and himself as the least in his father's house. He saw himself as the least of the least. God, however, did not see Gideon in this light. What He saw was Gideon's potential, the man he would become. This is why He called Gideon a "mighty man of valor" (vs. 12). Whenever Gideon looked in the mirror he saw someone insignificant, unimportant, and irrelevant yet God saw him as a great and mighty warrior. In no way did Gideon look like a mighty warrior, but God saw what he could be and what he would be. He saw what He intended to make him. Never let your circumstances and the opinion of others distort how you see yourself because they can't distort how God sees you. No matter how bad you've messed up in the past, God still sees a masterpiece, a divine work of art. He sees your value and the person He created you to be. Celebrate knowing that God sees the best in you always. He sees your potential.

Ps. 103:6 (MSG) says, "God makes everything come out right; He puts victims back on their feet." Your potential is there. God sees it and so should you. Each day He's making you better and better. Daily what you are becoming will be seen by many. Stop judging yourself by what you see today. God isn't finished yet. Phil. 1:6 (MSG), "The God who started this great work in you will keep at it and bring it to a flourishing finish." Think about it. You have God's word that He will finish what He started in you. His Word assures you that He will faithfully carry His work in you to completion. Don't give up and don't get discouraged. After all, Rome wasn't built in a day. No, this isn't easy. Things that are worthwhile rarely are. The good news is that God is still on the throne and He's molding you into the man of valor He wants you to be. 1 Peter 5:10 (AMP), "After you have suffered for a little while, the God of all grace will Himself complete, confirm, strengthen, and establish you, making you what you ought to be."

The Message Bible says, "It won't be long before this generous God who has great plans for us in Christ, will have you put together and on your feet for good. He gets the last word; yes, He does." With faith and patience let God finish the work He's started in you. God's power is at work to make you great so don't let doubt delay your transformation. Rejoice and be glad that each and every day your potential is coming to fruition more and more. Life is a journey so enjoy the daily step-by-step process. God's plan is always the best so trust the process. He knows how valuable you are. He sees your potential so rejoice knowing He has a great plan for your life. Author Zero Dean said, "Don't squander your potential living a life that amounts to far less than the one you are capable of living." Potential is a priceless treasure, an invaluable asset, a diamond in the rough waiting to shine. The big challenge is to become all that you have the possibility of becoming.

There is no heavier burden than unfulfilled potential. Henry Ford once said, "There is no man living who isn't capable of doing more than he thinks he can do." John Maxwell said, "Successful and unsuccessful people do not vary greatly in their abilities. They vary in their desire to reach their potential." There is so much more to life than what you see on the outside. The potential to be great is within and you must decide to unleash that potential to the fullest. To unlock your potential is going to require practice, consistency, and patience. Continuous effort is the key to unlocking your potential. Action breeds potential and potential changes the world. Just know that potential means nothing if you don't do anything with it. Author Taro Jaye Frank said, "People don't get promoted for doing their jobs really well. They get promoted by demonstrating their potential to do more." Faithfulness in your current assignment matters, but God looks beyond your present performance and sees the potential He placed within you.

Journalist Eric Burns said, "Greatness is more than potential. It is the execution of that potential. You need the discipline, the inspiration, the drive." Potential is inside of you and you must strive to get it out. Bodybuilder Andre Ferguson said, "Once I got a glimpse of my potential, the desire to be great was born." Stretch yourself to the limit and let God use you to the fullest. Charles Stanley said, "Your potential is the sum of all the possibilities God has for your life." Unleash your potential and put yourself in a place where God can use you. Be like Abraham Lincoln who said, "I will prepare and some day my chance will come." The parable of the mustard seed is about the power of potential and how it is birthed. Much can be learned from this short but powerful teaching. Jesus said, "The kingdom of God is like a mustard seed which a man took and sowed in the field" (Matt. 13:31). "It is the smallest of all seeds, but it becomes the largest of garden plants. It grows into a tree, and birds come and make nests in its branches" (vs. 32).

Greatness starts in obscurity. People may not always see your potential for greatness. This parable teaches us that something small and insignificant can become large and significant. Zech. 4:10 (NLT) says, "Do not despise small beginnings, for the Lord rejoices to see the work begin." In other words, it's not how you start that matters, it's how you finish. Whatever your circumstances, whatever the kingdom task that looms before you, don't despise the fact that your initial efforts seem small and insignificant. Don't get discouraged and don't belittle yourself. You may start out doing small things but in time your potential will allow a glorious manifestation of God's glory to shine forth. Regardless of where you are today, your best days are ahead of you. Job 8:7 says, "Though your beginning was small, yet your latter end will increase abundantly." If you find yourself in a small place today and your situation may be anything but great, then by faith keep looking up knowing your situation is only temporary.

Keep pressing into the great future prepared for you by God. Your situation is subject to change and God will cause your light and greatness to spring forth speedily (Is. 58:8). God destined you for greatness when He created you. Yes, He allows small beginnings but promises a great ending. Never forget that. Look what happened with Jesus. The angel Gabriel announced to Mary that her Son would be great, yet His beginning was in a remote manger (Luke 1:32). Consider David who was destined to be king in Israel but was a shepherd boy for many years. But he had a promise from God that he continually held onto. Likewise, there is a call on your life to be great. Yes, you are called to be exceptionally outstanding in the divine purpose God designed for your life. Just know that God is not intimidated by small starts. In fact, He ordains them. He shapes your character, strengthens your faith, and trains your heart through seasons where progress seems modest and fruit seems faint.

Small beginnings are where trust is built. This is where roots grow deep. Know with certainty that God never leaves His work unfinished. What begins in obscurity will end in glory. What starts in weakness will finish in strength. What looks like "not enough" will become "more than enough" once His hand touches it. So don't despise your small beginning. Don't be discouraged by slow steps or humble starts. God is writing a story that ends with victory, fulfillment, and overflow. If He began it, He will complete it. If He planted it, He will grow it. If He promised it, He will perform it. Once God's purpose is revealed to you, the journey toward the conquest of your destiny is set in motion and before long greatness is manifested in your life. You must step into your destiny. You must journey to that particular place in time where your greatness can shine forth and impact others. The journey to greatness makes you the person you are called to become. It molds you into your God-given identity.

Your destiny, which was sealed before time began, will shape you and develop you. And once you are developed by destiny, greatness is fulfilled. This is why you must dedicate all your time and energy to the pursuit of greatness. You need to make proper preparations to develop greatness. Manage your time well. Never allow people or things to consume the time needed for greatness. Time is one of the greatest gifts God has placed in your hands. It is the one resource you can never recover once it is spent. Scripture reminds us to "redeem the time, because the days are evil" (Eph. 5:16). That means your hours, your focus, and your energy are all sacred. They are tools meant to shape the calling God has placed on your life. Don't allow unnecessary distractions, people with no vision, or situations with no purpose to consume the time needed for your greatness. The enemy doesn't have to destroy you; he only needs to distract you, to pull your attention away from the things of God.

Every moment you waste is a moment you could have used to grow, to build, to pray, to develop, to serve, to prepare. Greatness requires discipline. Purpose requires intention. Destiny requires strict stewardship. Your future is shaped by what you choose to invest your time in today. So set your priorities. Guard your schedule. Learn to say no to what drains you so you can say yes to what God is calling you to. Surround yourself with people who feed your spirit, not just your emotions. Protect your mind from the noise. Make room for prayer. Make room for growth. Make room for greatness. When you value your time, you honor the God who gave it to you. Your destiny deserves your focus. Your calling deserves your commitment. Your greatness deserves your time. Learn to listen to God for it has an eternal effect on your destiny. Ps. 73:24 (NLT) says, "You guide me with Your counsel, leading me to a glorious destiny." God's guidance lights the way, leading you to the destiny He's prepared.

God's plan and purpose for your life are seeds of greatness that has been placed in you and it's your responsibility to germinate them into action. Be faithful and determined not to leave this planet until you have developed all the potential for greatness that God has given you. God knows your potential otherwise He would not have put those seeds there. He knew those seeds have the potential to sprout, grow, and produce good fruit in your life. Each seed of greatness in you has the potential to become a tree which has the potential to become a huge forest because of the seeds within that one tree. Like that tree, your potential is limitless. With God by your side all things are possible. There is no limit to what God can do in your life if you let

Him. Trust God to increase your greatness in every area of life. Don't settle for just being good because being good is the enemy of being great. God promised you greatness and He won't have you accept anything less than that.

Passionately ask God to increase your greatness. This is a prayer He longs to answer. Greatness is all over you. God sees your greatness and the devil sees your greatness. It is now time for you to see just how great you truly are. Live your life knowing that when you walk into a room greatness shows up with you. Now that you have arrived nothing will be the same. The word "great" means 'above the normal or average ability, quality, or distinction.' Praise God, you are not normal or average. You are great! Every man has a purpose, a destiny to fulfill. Greatness is when you achieve the reason for which you were created and maximize its influence in the lives of others. God has destined every man to be great, to be outstanding in whatever they do. A great man is a person whose life blesses other people. To be great is magnificent. It's the quality of being distinguished, renowned, preeminent, notable, prestigious, important, significant, and influential.

Being great is a position of power and respect, of being larger than the ordinary, to be outstanding and remarkable. Greatness is God's advertising His power in and through your life. You are not here merely to occupy space in this world; you are here to impact the world. And with the God-given potential inside of you, you can do just that. To change the world you live in, you must know what your potential is because you can't use what you don't know you have. Your birth and your existence have been intentionally orchestrated by God. The day He formed you in your mother's womb He placed inside you great potential. With this potential you are able to fulfill and carry out your God-given assignment. This, in turn, will bring you rich fulfillment, happiness, and inner satisfaction. The potential God placed inside of you aligns with the purpose He has given you to fulfill and carry out. Your potential and your purpose go hand-in-hand. If you're not utilizing all your potential, you're not fulfilling all your purpose.

Getting saved is not a stopping point, it's a starting line. It's when you have the desire to see God do great things not just for you but through you. Take your potential and like an arrow aim it in the direction of your destiny, not in the area of your distraction. Take aim and take action. Your potential is limitless when the power of God is working in your life. Power is exciting. Great crowds followed Jesus to see the demonstration of God's supernatural power. Paul writes, "Be strong in the Lord and in the power of His might" (Eph. 6:10). With this power mountains will be cast into the sea and oceans will part. Jesus said, "Nothing will be impossible for you" (Matt. 17:20) when you operate in the power of His name and in the power of His blood. The fact that you were born is proof that God knew you had the potential to accomplish a divine assignment. Don't go to your grave with your talents not used. Act upon your dreams. Believe the power of God in your life. Reach for greatness.

Dare to fly on the wings of faith and live your life with no limitations. Consider your potential in God. He has given you dominion over all the earth (Gen. 1:26). He's made you to be kings and priests unto Him (Rev. 1:6). The Holy Spirit dwells in you and you are joint heirs with the Lord Jesus Christ. You talk to God and He talks to you. You decrease so He might increase. You are a child of God and great is your potential. You see the invisible, you hear the inaudible, you know the unknowable, you do the impossible. Enjoy the journey of life as you walk hand-in-hand with the King of kings and Lord of lords. His greatness is in you, and this is what activates your potential. Use faith to release your potential. Without faith it's impossible to please God (Heb. 11:6). The just shall live by faith (Heb. 10:38) for it is the victory that has overcome the world (1 John 5:4). Faith is not an option, it's a requirement. Faith does not demand miracles, it creates miracles. Faith is not a leap in the dark; it's a walk in the light.

Jesus said, "Whatever you ask in My name, I will do it" (John 14:13,14). Believe that and there will be no limit to what your potential can accomplish. The unprofitable servant who buried his one talent because he was afraid was cast into outer darkness with much weeping and gnashing of teeth (Matt. 25:30). Why did this happen? Because he didn't maximize his full potential. The potential was there but he buried it and paid a heavy price for what he did. Cast your fear aside and press on anyway. You will learn quickly that the pain of falling short is nothing compared to the shame of stopping short. Give it all you've got. Go the extra mile and then some. As you do that, your potential will kick in and great things will begin to happen. Give God your two fish and five loaves and watch it get multiplied over and over again. Great is your potential when you place it in the hands of God. Run after your potential for it's what gives you the possibility of progress. This is what causes you to get up each and every morning.

| 6 |

"SPIRITUAL PASSION"

The God who spoke worlds into existence and flung stars into space is the same God who fearfully and wonderfully made you and filled you with greatness. Your greatness, your courage, the hero in you, comes from your Father in heaven above who is the giver of every good and perfect gift (James 1:17). He knows your potential. This is why He encourages you to dream big, to pursue what He put in your heart, to allow the gifts He put in you to come out. God places dreams in our hearts - visions that often feel bigger than ourselves. He doesn't give them to intimidate us; He gives them to inspire us. Every gift He has placed within you, every passion, every idea, is a divine seed. He encourages you to dream boldly, to step beyond comfort and fear, and to pursue the path He has prepared for you. When you act on the gifts He's given, you honor Him. When you step into the dreams He's planted, you allow His light to shine through you in ways the world desperately needs.

Trust that He equips those He calls. Let your heart be fearless, your steps intentional, and your vision limitless, for the Creator of the universe delights in seeing His children rise and fulfill the extraordinary purposes He designed for them. Remember that God's dreams for you are never too big because He is bigger. Your gifts are never too small because His Spirit is greater. Let Him guide you, and watch as what He has placed in you comes alive, transforming not only your life but the lives of everyone around you. Now is the time to let your greatness show, the time to shine and go further than others thought, to accomplish dreams bigger than they could ever imagine. Greatness gives you the confidence to know that He "who began a good work in you will continue His work until it is finally finished on the day when Christ Jesus returns" (Phil. 1:6). This confidence will cause you to step into a new sense of boldness that will see God's favor and power increase mightily in your life.

You are God's masterpiece. He equipped you, empowered you, and anointed you. He put seeds of greatness in you that will propel you to the top of the mountain. Don't look around you but look up to your Heavenly Father who is the giver of big gifts, big favor, and bigger and greater opportunities. He'll give you the creativity to do great things. Trust God who said in Is. 43:19, "Behold, I will do a new thing; now it shall spring forth; shall you not know it? I will even make a way in the wilderness, and rivers in the desert." Keep dreaming and keep believing because the greatness in you is about to spring forth. Enlarge your vision and God will use you to do great things on the earth. God never designed your life to be small, limited, or confined by fear, past failures, or the expectations of others. Before God does something great through a person, He first expands that person's vision. What you see determines what you pursue. What you expect determines what you receive.

Potential is what God sees when He looks at you. He sees who you can be in Him. The good news is He'll never leave you the way He found you. Potential takes you from where you are to the place God wants you to be. It takes you out of the valley and places you on the mountain of success and greatness. John Maxwell said, "The word 'potential' is one of the most wonderful words in any language. It looks forward with optimism. It is filled with hope. It promises success. It implies fulfillment. It hints at greatness. It is a word based on possibilities. Do you have potential? Absolutely." When you see your potential, you see the possibilities before you. You see a higher ceiling, a higher level of your involvement in the kingdom of God. Ps. 1:3 (NLT) says, "They are like trees planted along the riverbank, bearing fruit each season. Their leaves never whither, and they prosper in all they do." That's potential!

The Message Bible says, "You're a tree replanted in Eden, bearing fresh fruit every month, never dropping a leaf, always in blossom." A tree represents vitality and fruitfulness, strength and endurance. So should every man be. The GWT says, "He succeeds in everything he does." A tree is upright and grows upward toward heaven. A planted tree is under the care and cultivation of its owner who is God Himself. The roots of a tree are refreshed by never ending streams of living water. A tree grows tall and strong because of the life flowing from its roots. Great men stand tall for God. They are strong and well-rooted in God's Word. They are unmovable in times of trial and temptation. Just as healthy trees add a new ring of growth each year, men who are great continually "grow in the grace and knowledge of our Lord and Savior" (2 Peter 3:18). A tree planted by water has everything it needs to grow and become strong and solid. It has all the potential it needs to do what God created it to do.

Some trees provide food, other give shade, others are made into lumber. Likewise, all men are to provide spiritual food, shelter, and comfort to those around them. Isaiah refers to great men when he writes, "They will be called oaks of righteousness, a planting of the Lord for the display of His splendor" (Is. 61:3 NIV). The NLT says, "They will be like great oaks that the Lord has planted for His own glory." Your calling as a man is to flourish so God can be glorified. In a world filled with dead trees, the great men of God should be like a large, vibrant oak tree, flourishing with righteous works that glorify God. Jesus said, "Let your light shine before men in such a way that they may see your good works and glorify your Father who is in heaven" (Matt. 5:16). A great man is solid and righteous through and through. He is strong and endures the storms of life. He will "flourish like a palm tree and grow like a cedar in Lebanon" (Ps. 92:12).

Charles Spurgeon said, "The righteous shall flourish like a palm tree, whose growth may not be so rapid, but whose endurance for centuries is in fine contrast with the transitory verdure of the meadow. When we see a noble palm standing erect, sending all its strength upward in one bold column, and growing amid the drought of the desert, we have a fine picture of a godly man, a man who aims alone at the glory of God and, independent of outward circumstances, is made by divine grace to live and thrive where all things else perish. On the summit of the mountain the cedar waves its mighty branches in splendor and majesty, and so the truly godly man under all adversities retain the joy of his soul." Men who are great dwell in habitual fellowship with God and become men of full spiritual growth. They are rich in grace, happy in experience, and mighty in influence. They bring forth fruit in old age. Nature decays but grace thrives. "Though our outer man is decaying, our inner man is being renewed day by day" (2 Cor. 4:16).

When men grow old and become weak in themselves, they become strong in the Lord and abound in bearing fruit that is acceptable to God. The weakness of the body does not diminish the strength of the spirit. In fact, it is often in the fading of natural strength that the power of God shines brightest. As the years pass, human ability, confidence, and vigor naturally diminish. The hands that once worked tirelessly grow slower, the legs that once carried miles grow weary, and the voice that once thundered with strength may soften. Yet God, in His infinite wisdom, designed our journey so that the decline of human strength becomes the doorway to divine strength. For the believer, old age is not a season of loss - it is a season of exchange. The Apostle Paul teaches that "though our outward man perish, yet the inward man is renewed day by day" (2 Cor. 4:16). As our dependence on self fades, our dependence on God deepens. As the flesh weakens, the spirit becomes more sensitive to the presence and power of the Lord.

However feeble his outward man may be, the true man of God is fresh and flourishing. He is like a tree that is full of sap and bears luxurious foliage. He's like a tree planted by water whose leaf does not whither. He brings forth fruit in its season and whatever he does shall prosper no matter what his age is. Being old didn't stop Abraham from having a child at the age of one hundred and it didn't stop Caleb from going to war on a mountain full of giants. To them, age was just a number. It is often the aged saint - leaning on a cane, walking slowly, speaking gently - whose prayers shake heaven and whose faith moves mountains. Their bodies may be frail, but their roots run deep. Their confidence is no longer in themselves, but in the God who has carried them through every valley and lifted them upon every mountain. And it is in this season that they bear their sweetest fruit. Not the fruit of physical accomplishments, but the fruit of righteousness, wisdom, patience, and love.

Like an old tree whose branches may be weathered but whose fruit is richer than ever, the elderly believer stands as a testimony that spiritual fruitfulness does not diminish with age - it increases. The spiritual fragrance of their life touches families, inspires churches, and points hearts to Christ. In God's kingdom, weakness is never the end. It is the place where divine strength begins. For when we become weak in ourselves, we become strong in the Lord. And when we lean wholly upon Him, we abound in fruit that glorifies His name. No matter what your age may be, you should always seek greatness. Embrace it. Do not be passive. Do not be a bystander who does nothing. With passion and purpose bring the kingdom of God to those around you. Greatness involves dreaming big. Great men are motivated by dreams which are beyond their capacity to fulfill, by dreams that are bigger than they are.

To be great you must be diligent and persistent in all you do. Prov. 22:29 says a diligent man "will stand before kings; he will not stand before unknown men." A diligent man is not discouraged by any obstacle or barrier. With grit and great determination he pursues his goals until his destiny is fulfilled. Don't bury that seed of greatness. When you nurture it and grow it you will flourish like a palm tree and grow like a cedar in Lebanon. Cedar trees were very important in biblical times. They were majestic, stable, durable, and incorruptible. Be diligent and this is how you will be. Desire is a key to greatness. To be great, you must desire to be great. Desire is a key that God Himself placed in the human heart. It is the spark that ignites purpose, the inward fire that moves a person from where they are to where God is calling them to be. Before greatness is ever seen by men, it is first stirred by God in the hidden chambers of the soul.

The Lord never forces greatness on anyone; He invites us into it. He plants the seed, but He waits for desire to water it. Desire is what caused Abraham to look for a city whose builder and maker is God. Desire is what pushed David from shepherd's fields to a king's throne. Desire is what caused Paul to cry out, "I press toward the mark..." Every person God lifted had something burning in them - a refusal to remain where they were, and a deep longing to grow, to stretch, to rise, and to glorify God through their lives. Greatness begins when you say in your heart, "Lord, make me into what You have created me to be." It continues when you nurture that desire with prayer, obedience, discipline, and faith. And it becomes reality when your desire aligns fully with God's will. So do not shrink back from desiring greatness. Desire to be great in faith. Desire to be great in love. Desire to be great in obedience. Desire to be great in the calling He placed upon you. The moment desire wakes up in your spirit; heaven begins to move in your direction.

Desire is born out of need and dissatisfaction with your present position. Desire is what gives birth to miracles. Mark 11:24 says, "Whatever things you desire when you pray, believe that you receive them and you will have them." Greatness also comes through obedience, when you're willing to do what God instructed you to do. Abraham obeyed and God made his name great (Gen. 12:2). Faith is a vital key to greatness. What you do not believe, you cannot be empowered to become. Unshakable faith will propel you on your way to greatness. The greatest enemy to unlocking your potential is complacency. God said in Zeph. 1:12, "At that time I will search Jerusalem and punish the men who are settled in complacency." The word "complacency" means 'to be pleased with oneself or one's merits, advantages, and situation without the awareness of some potential danger to being self-satisfied.'

When you become complacent you let your guard down and your discernment is weakened. You're so comfortable in a situation you don't know that danger is lurking nearby. Men who are complacent have no desire to expand their horizons. Their satisfaction with their own abilities prevents them from trying harder. They're overly content to stay in their self-made comfort zone. Their expectations are lowered, and their convictions are easily compromised. They're content to flock around with a bunch of chickens when they have the potential to rise up and soar like a mighty eagle. The careless ease of how they approach life will eventually lead to their downfall. Prov. 1:32 (NLT) says, "Fools are destroyed by their own complacency." That means destruction doesn't always come suddenly; sometimes it comes quietly, gradually, and subtly, through the unnoticed comfort of spiritual stagnation. Bible translator James Moffatt said, "For heedless folk fall by their own self-will, the senseless are destroyed by their indifference."

Men who are complacent turn away from the voice of wisdom. They are self-deceived because their excessive unconcern for life gives them a false sense of peace. Their smugness and lack of anxiety will destroy them. Zeph. 1:12 (MSG) says, "I'll find and punish those who are sitting it out, fat and lazy, amusing themselves and taking it easy." Is. 32:11 (NIV) says, "Tremble, you complacent women; shudder, you daughters who feel secure." The NCV says, "You are calm now, but you should shake with fear." Spiritual apathy, coldness, and indifference will destroy your potential. Helen Keller said, "One can never consent to creep when one feels an impulse to soar." Men who are great don't get complacent but day by day have a renewed spiritual fervency that allows them to soar on the wind currents of the Holy Spirit. Spiritual passion is more than an emotion. It's a fire that keeps drawing us back to God. It's the state of wanting to hear His voice each and every day.

When men get complacent, like a mother eagle God will push them out of their nest of comfort. He loves us too much to let us sleep through our purpose and be inactive in our calling. He's nudging you out of the nest so you can soar to the place where His blessings will overtake you, to the place where He can use you for His glory. Webster's Dictionary defines "complacency" as 'a feeling of being satisfied with how things are and not wanting to try to make them better.' When men fail to take the time to access, process, and see the horizon ahead, they become complacent with where they are and lose sight of where God wants them to go. To combat complacency you must forever be keeping company with God. There should always be a constant divine conversation going on between you and your Heavenly Father. God wants to lead you and give you divine direction by His Spirit. This can only happen if you make it a daily habit to talk to Him and actively listen to Him.

There is always a next step in your journey to fulfill your destiny. We are pilgrims in a strange land and we must forever be going forward while we are here. As followers of Christ, we must never forget that this world is not our home. Scripture calls us "strangers and pilgrims." We are people passing through a land that is not our final destination. We are here with purpose, but we are not here to stay. Heaven is our homeland, and every step we take on this earth is meant to lead us closer to the One who called us. Pilgrims do not settle. They do not plant their roots in the soil of temporary things. They walk with intention, with eyes lifted toward the promise ahead. In the same way, we are called to keep moving forward - growing in grace, deepening our faith, and refusing to let the world shape us into its image. There will be valleys along the way, and mountains that seem too high to climb but pilgrims press on. They travel with faith as their compass and hope as their strength.

While we are here, let us walk forward with courage. Let us cast off anything that slows us, anything that dims our devotion, anything that distracts us from Christ. Keep your heart set on things above. Keep your feet pointed toward the Kingdom. Keep your spirit marching on, even when the road is rough. The enemy of your soul wants to stop this journey all together and he'll use complacency to take you off the path you're supposed to be on. To combat complacency you must take action. You need to walk forward in confidence knowing God is with you every step of the way. You must get out of your comfort zone. Amos 6:1 says, "Woe to you who are at ease in Zion." MSG, "Woe to you who think you live on easy street in Zion." Consider Abraham who would never had discovered God's amazing plans for his life unless he was first willing to leave the safety of a familiar and secure place. The disciples would have always been just another bunch of fishermen unless they have been willing to abandon the security of their career for the call of Jesus.

Your potential lies beyond your comfort zone. Your destiny will only be fulfilled if and only if you move beyond the security blanket and abandon yourself to total trust in God. Don't let being comfortable, complacency, and carelessness kill your calling. Stop procrastinating! Just because an opportunity comes your way does not mean it will come again. Complacency is the enemy of security and progress. Canadian writer Robin Sharma said, "The discomfort of change is better than the heartbreak of complacency." The tragedy of life is not found in failure but in complacency. Not in doing too much but doing too little. Not in living above your means, but below your potential. John Maxwell said, "Of all the things a leader should fear, complacency heads the list." Yes, complacency is man's biggest weakness. It creeps upon you when you least expect it. Complacency saps your energy, dulls your attitude, and drains your brain. It makes you satisfied with the way things are, and it rejects the things that might be.

Do not let complacency destroy your life. Instead, do what the Lord said in Amos 5:4, "Seek Me and live." This is truly the cry of God's heart. These four words is God's invitation to return to a pure and genuine devotion to Him. God is our "fountain of life" (Ps. 36:9) and from Him we "draw water from the wells of salvation" (Ps. 12:3). Wholehearted pursuit is the key to life with God. Jer. 29:13 says, "You will seek Me and find Me when you seek Me with all your heart." Seek God and live. Fulfilling your destiny happens when you take bold, massive, and specific action. Gradual and timid change will lead you to draw back into your comfort zone. It's nearly impossible to move forward without a committed and courageous lead. May your hunger for change be greater than your complacency to stay the same. There is no limit to what you can accomplish if you will learn to shake off complacency and keep stretching to the next level.

| 7 |

"THE STARTING POINT"

To be great you must have a God-inspired imagination. You need to let God expand the way you think because your imagination shapes your life. Greatness never begins on the outside - it starts in the unseen places of the mind and heart. Before God ever brings you into your destiny, He first transforms the way you think. Your imagination is not a toy or a distraction; it is one of the greatest spiritual tools God has given you. It is the canvas where faith paints possibility. When your imagination is small, your life will stay small. When your thoughts are confined, your future becomes confined. But when God breathes on your imagination - when He enlarges your vision, expands your perspective, and stretches your expectations - then you begin to see the world the way He sees it. And nothing is impossible with God. Abraham had to imagine himself as the father of many nations before Isaac was ever born. David had to imagine victory over Goliath before he ever ran onto the battlefield.

God always plants greatness in your imagination long before you ever walk in it. This is why Scripture tells us to "be transformed by the renewing of your mind" (Rom. 12:2). God doesn't start by changing your circumstances; He starts by changing your inner vision. He expands your thinking, enlarges your faith, and fills your imagination with His promises. When you allow God to shape the pictures in your mind, your life begins to move in the direction of His plan. So don't be afraid to dream big, pray boldly, and imagine the impossible. Let God inspire the pictures you hold inside your heart. As your imagination grows, your capacity grows. As your vision expands, your future opens. Greatness is not achieved by human effort alone - it is birthed in a God-inspired imagination, Let God enlarge your thinking, and you will find yourself stepping into the greatness He has already prepared for you.

The way you think will affect the way you feel and the way you feel will affect the way you act. Prov. 23:7 says, "For as a man thinks in his heart, so is he." Prov. 4:23 (ICB) says, "Be very careful about what you think. Your thoughts run your life." The TEV says, "Your life is shaped by your thoughts." Imagination is the force that trespasses on the impossible. Napolean Bonaparte said, "Imagination rules the world." Philosopher Pascal said, "Imagination decides everything." With your imagination you see God's plan and purpose for your life. What you see and your pursuit of it is what's supposed to dominate your life. It's the reason you were born. A supernatural imagination will stretch beyond the limitations of the natural world. It will take you into the heavenly realm where greatness rules supreme. God is forever talking to you but you'll never hear what He's saying until you first see with your imagination what He's saying.

You will not exercise your faith until you first see a picture of what you're believing for. When you hear God speak, your response should be, "I see what You're saying." The creative ability to use your imagination was given to you by God as a way of empowering you to bring to pass whatever you can imagine. J. K. Rowling said, "We do not need magic to transform our world. We carry all of the power we need inside ourselves already." That power is your imagination. 2 Cor. 4:18 says, "We do not look at the things which are seen, but at the things which are not seen." How can you look at things which are not seen? Only with your imagination. Imagination is where the conception takes place. If you can't see it on the inside, you won't ever see it on the outside. Albert Einstein once said, "Imagination is everything. It is the preview to life's coming attractions." In other words, what you see in your imagination is what you'll get.

Science will tell you that your mind can't tell the difference between real experiences and one that is vividly and repeatedly imagined. To your mind, they're both one and the same. Men perform and behave not in accordance with reality, but in accordance with their imagined perception of reality. What you imagine will become your reality. Everything you see in this world came from somebody's imagination. Like faith, imagination is the evidence of things not seen. When you imagine something good, it's actually God giving you a preview of a coming attraction He has planned for your life. In other words, your future is found in the things you imagine today. The bigger your imagination, the bigger and brighter your future will be. Men who are great imagine what could be and what will be while living in the present. Francis Schaeffer said a man's imagination "should fly beyond the stars." Imagination unlocks impossibilities. It's a tool by which you cooperate with God to participate in His divine nature and fulfill your God-given purpose.

A sure sign that God is not through with you is that He wakes you up each morning. When He's done with you, you won't wake up no more. The very fact that you are awake shows there is more God has in store for your life. To help show you what that is, He has given you a divine imagination. God has a big plan for your life. 1 Cor. 2:9 (NLT) says, "No eyes has seen, no ear heard and no mind has imagined what God has prepared for those who love Him." Paul is telling us that God's plans for His people surpass human senses, human imagination, and human limitation. What God is preparing for you is not confined to what you have experienced, what others have told you, or what you can conceive in your greatest moment of faith. His thoughts are higher, His purposes deeper, and His blessings richer than anything you've ever known. God's plan for your life is mind-boggling. Eph. 3:20 (NCV) says, "With God's power working in us God can do much more than anything we can ask or imagine."

Even your boldest dreams and your strongest moments of faith cannot fully grasp what God has prepared. What He has planned will exceed expectations, overturn limitations, and overwhelm you with His goodness. God is a big God and the secret to success is to let the size of your God determine the size of your dream. You need to let God stretch your imagination. When you wake up each morning, ask God to open up your imagination. Dream big dreams and then pursue them with everything you've got. Stretch your imagination and watch what God will do for you. Your life will never be the same. You'll soar high above the mediocre world we live in. Faith is when you let God stretch your imagination. Ask Him to let you see the things He sees; to let you see the glorious future He has planned for your life. Caleb stretched his imagination when he stood up and said, "Let us go up at once and take possession, for we are well able to overcome it" (Num. 13:30).

Caleb's imagination made him a great man. He saw the people defeating the giants who lived there. He imagined them enjoying the land flowing with milk and honey. For sure, one of the greatest gifts God has given man is the gift of imagination. It's the ability to see things, to think and create with mental pictures in your mind. Your imagination is a gift from God to be used for His good purposes. Use this gift to create an image of the future, to see yourself becoming great and doing great things. Your imagination is a tool God has given you to see His will manifested in your life. With it comes the power to move mountains and to fulfill your destiny. Your imagination allows you to see into your future, to see your life and circumstances through the eyes of God, to see His supernatural power working in your life. Imagination visualizes what faith knows to be true. It's faith that calls us to imagine. It gives us assurance about things we cannot see

God said about the people of Babel, "This is only the beginning of what they will do. Now nothing they have imagined they can do will be impossible for them!" (Gen. 11:6). What God is saying is there is power in your imagination. He wants you to know that great lives are built around great dreams and great imaginations. Not earthly fantasies, not self-made ambitions but God-breathed visions that lift you above the ordinary and pull you into the extraordinary purpose He designed for you. From the very beginning, God has used imagination - holy, Spirit-inspired imagination - to reveal His plans to His people. He gave Abraham a vision of stars in the sky. He gave Joseph dreams that shaped nations. He showed Moses a Promised Land before Moses ever set foot in it. Every great work of God began with someone willing to see beyond what their eyes could see. Let God expand your imagination. Let Him enlarge your dreams. Let Him show you what He have prepared for your life.

It is impossible to be great without having a great dream. To be great you must unlock your imagination and see God using you to do great things. Dream big and visualize God using you in a mighty way. Eph. 1:18 (NJB) says, "May God enlighten the eyes of your mind so that you can see the hope that His calling holds for you." The "eyes of your mind" is your imagination. To be great your imagination must come alive. You must see by faith God's plan and purpose for your life. Developing an imagination is a necessity to walking in faith. Your faith needs imagination as much as your imagination needs faith. Imagination transcends intellect and what we can feel and hold. Logic may change our mind but it's the interplay between imagination and faith that changes our life. Albert Einstein said, "Imagination is more important than knowledge. Logic will get you from A to B. Imagination will take you everywhere." He also said, "The true sign of intelligence is not knowledge but imagination."

George Bernard Shaw said, "Imagination is the beginning of creation." Men who are great empower their imagination and see what God wants them to do. Prov. 29:18 says, "Where there is no vision, the people perish." Where there is no vision the people cast off restraint (NIV), they run wild (TLB), are uncontrolled (BBE), become demoralized (NAB), they get out of hand (NJB). Get a vision of God's dream for your life. It's bigger, far larger, and eternally more significant than any dream you can come up with on your own. Eph. 3:20 (MSG), "God can do anything, you know, far more than you could ever imagine or guess or request in your wildest dreams!" God's plan for your life is huge! It's enormous! Don't limit what He can do by thinking small. Use the imagination He gave you and dream big dreams. Dreaming big honors God. It shows that you trust Him, that you have faith in His willingness and ability to cause His plan for your life to come to pass.

You will need faith to become great for without faith it is impossible to please God (Heb. 11:6). However, on the journey to greatness, faith is not where you start. The starting point is your imagination. It's the tool God has given you to create a bigger and brighter future for yourself, a tool that will help make you great. Pablo Picasso said, "Everything you can imagine is real." Carl Sagan said, "Imagination will often carry us to worlds that never were, but without it we go nowhere." Gen. 1:27 says, "So God created man in His own image." The word "image" is the root word of "imagination." In the imagination of God, He created man. Novelist Henry Miller said, "Imagination is the voice of daring. If there is anything Godlike about God it is that He dared to imagine everything." This tells us that the role, the purpose, of imagination is to create things. God told Abraham to look at the stars and said, "So shall your descendants be" (Gen. 15:5).

God used the image of the stars to fuel Abraham's imagination. If he didn't have an image of where God was taking him, he'd go back to where he used to be. During times of trial and despair, all Abraham had to do was look up at the night sky. All those stars ignited the flickering flame of his imagination. When in doubt, use your imagination to put you back on the right path. God's imagination created us. We're created in His image; therefore, we can also create with our imagination. Mark Twain said, "Reality can be beaten with enough imagination." He also said, "You can't depend on your eyes when your imagination is out of focus." A man's greatest power is his imagination. Without it he will achieve nothing. Muhammad Ali said, "The man who has no imagination has no wings." Imagination plays a great role and has much value in a man's life. Men who continually use the power of a great imagination are the ones who are changing the world.

Men who are great make their dreams come true. They believe in the power of their imagination and see the possibilities before them. Faith is the vehicle that takes you to your future and imagination is the engine of faith. If you don't use your imagination, your faith will sit idle and take you nowhere. This is why God wants to ignite your imagination. He wants you to imagine the impossible taking place in your life. You don't have to make it happen; you just have to imagine it. God said to Abraham in Gen. 12:2, "And I will make you a great nation, and I will bless you and make your name great; and you shall be a blessing." Notice that Abraham never asked God to make him great. He never prayed, "Lord, exalt my name," or "Make me famous in the earth." His greatness was God's idea. Abraham's part was not to scheme or struggle for greatness. His part was to believe, to imagine, and to see himself as God described him because faith begins in the heart long before it appears in the world.

It was impossible for Abraham to have a son in his old age, but he looked up at the stars and imagined it anyway. He imagined God doing the impossible. Luke 1:37 (AMP) says, "For with God nothing is ever impossible and no word from God shall be without power or impossible of fulfillment." Abraham became great because of his imagination and his faith. Through both of them working together he received the power to fulfill his God-given destiny. Likewise, through the power of your imagination, nothing will be impossible to you. Goals get accomplished, dreams come true, and victories are celebrated. Imagination is the starting point of all achievement. Every dream and every goal started in the realm of a person's imagination. They imagined something and they made it real. Everything you see in this world came from someone's imagination. What is now real was once only an imagination.

There is so much power in a person's imagination and the people who do not believe in their imagination are, in truth, fools and cowards. Only men who are great and successful believe in the power of their imagination. The stronger your imagination, the greater you will be. It's your imagination that puts you on the road to victory and success. What you imagine can become real with faith and a whole lot of hard work and diligence. You can achieve everything you desire but you must first imagine it happening. That is when a supernatural power will awaken in your heart and soul. It is power that will show you countless possibilities that will turn your imagination into manifested reality so that your destiny will be fulfilled. If you'll start imagining now what you want to achieve or create, God will start showing you a path to take to reach your goal. Keep dreaming big dreams and imagine more and more. It requires a lot of determination and effort to become great but if it was easy everyone would be doing it.

Divine imagination is the most marvelous, miraculous, and inconceivably the most powerful force the world has ever known. It is the place where God whispers possibilities into the human heart. It is the sacred canvas where heaven paints its dreams and invites us to participate. Divine imagination is not fantasy; it is revelation. It is God showing you what can be through the eyes of faith. For sure, it is the greatest creative faculty you possess. Right now there is creative, unadulterated power flowing through you. It's the power of a godly imagination. Keep it active and use it daily. Your greatness depends on it. With divine imagination comes divine enablement. Open up and set free your anointed imagination and let it do the job it was created to do. Jesus said to enter the kingdom you must become like little children (Matt. 18:3). What do children have that most adults don't have? A vivid imagination. Children play with their friends and pretend they're great athletes, great soldiers, great pilots, great doctors, great superheroes.

A child's imagination knows no boundaries. When they dream, they reach beyond the clouds, soar past the stars, and imagine worlds we cannot yet see. Spiritually, this is a reminder of the limitless possibilities God places within each of us. Just as a child believes anything is possible, God invites us to trust in His vision for our lives. When we nurture wonder, faith, and creativity, we open ourselves to His boundless plan. Let your heart be like a child's - bold in dreams, fearless in faith, and limitless in hope - because with God, the sky is never the limit; it is just the beginning. Imagine the heights you can climb if you had the imagination of a young child. Nothing would stand in your way as you climb the ladder to greatness. How do you become great? Become more like a little child. Childlike faith coupled together with a childlike imagination will bring greatness into your life. Imagine yourself being unstoppable and unbeatable. Imagine yourself being all God created you to be.

| 8 |

"DIVINE CREATIVITY"

G od has placed within every man a powerful imagination -
a sacred canvas where dreams are painted, visions are
born, and possibilities are awakened. Imagination is not just a
human ability; it is a divine gift. It lets us see beyond what is
and glimpse what could be. Yet imagination alone is not
enough. Many can dream, but it takes divine creativity to bring
into manifestation those things you imagine taking place. Divine creativity is the breath of God moving upon the pictures
in your mind. Just as the Spirit hovered over the waters before
the world was formed, that same Spirit waits to hover over
your ideas, your hopes, your inner visions. When you surrender your imagination to Him, He takes what is abstract and
gives it structure, direction, and life. Your thoughts become
guided, your dreams become refined, and your creative power
becomes supernatural. Only those who invite God into the creative process can see those dreams manifested in the natural
world.

The first thing we learn about God is that He is a creator. Gen.1:1 says, "In the beginning God created the heavens and the earth." Creativity is one of the core characteristics of God (Rom. 1:20) and the concept of creativity is found in 60 of the 66 books of the Bible. Without God, imagination can inspire. But with God, imagination can create. What you see in your heart can become what you touch with your hands - not by striving, not by forcing, but by partnering with the Creator Himself. God doesn't just give you visions; He gives you the grace to bring them forth. He aligns opportunities, opens doors, and empowers you to act with wisdom and bold-ness. Creativity is so powerful that words such as 'create, make, form, designed' is found over a thousand times from Genesis to Revelation. Dream boldly, imagine freely, and more than anything, invite God into the process. Let His divine creativity flow through your mind, shape your vision, and bring forth manifestations that reveal His glory.

When your imagination is surrendered to God, it becomes more than a human ability - it becomes a tool of heaven cre-ating on earth what God has placed in your spirit. What God inspires, God empowers. What God shows, God brings to pass. And what God plants in your imagination, He desires to manifest in your life. It was creativity that brought Adam to life (Gen. 1:27). It was creativity that gives us breath (Gen. 2:7), that gave the animals their names (Gen. 2:19). It was creativity that invented clothing (Gen. 3:7), that caused a family to sur-vive a flood (Gen. 6:14), that scattered the nations and created different languages (Gen. 11:3). Creativity is everywhere in the Bible and in every single instance it's for, by, and from the purposes of God (Col. 1:16,17). It's from God and for God. We then learn that He made man in His own image (Gen. 1:26,27). This tells us that we were created to be a reflection of God's creativity. You're to show the world the goodness of God through the gift of creativity.

There is a call on your life beckoning you to step into the fullness of your creative potential. To be great you must unleash your God-given creativity. Creativity is a natural part of human expression that all men should value and cultivate. It helps you to think outside the box and find new solutions to problems. Creativity is a fundamental tool for success in every area of life. It empowers men who are great to push beyond the boundaries of what is already known. With hard work, faith, and a lot of patience, you'll be able to accurately capture and express what's in your creative imagination. Creativity comes from the heart, a place of emotion and inspiration. It's an endless resource that becomes more activated the more you unleash it. Creativity takes you above and beyond the norm as you explore new horizons and boldly go where no man has gone before. It calls you to explore new horizons - territories of faith, wisdom, and revelation that can only be discovered by those who dare to step out with God.

Every one of us is wonderfully unique, fashioned by God with a distinct blend of gifts, experiences, and inner vision. Because of this divine design, no two people think the same, see the same, or create the same. Creativity flows through the heart like living water, but it is your God-given individuality - your personality, talents, and perspective - that shapes that flow into something beautifully original. Creative ideas are not random thoughts; they are whispers of possibility filtered through the uniqueness God placed within you. The way you interpret a moment, the way you sense a problem, the way you imagine a solution are all expressions of your divine makeup. Others may see what you see, but no one can create what you create, because no one else carries your exact blend of insight and skill. Every man has his own frame of reference and viewpoint of the world which means that everyone has the potential to create something original.

Author Elizabeth Gilbert said, "A creative life is an amplified life. It's a bigger life, a happier life, an expanded life, and a lot more interesting life." Trust God and He'll enhance your creativity and make you a fountain of wisdom regarding those things that matter most in the world. He'll unlock the creativity inside of you and wisdom will start flowing into the lives of other people. They'll be greatly inspired by the things you have to say. Men who are great have the ability to think about a task or a problem in a new and different way. They have the ability to use their imagination to generate new ideas. When you are creative, you look at things from a unique perspective. The creative person thinks of ways to improve results and produce excellent work. Deep within every believer lies a wellspring of divine creativity - a sacred spark breathed into the inner man by God Himself - and you must consciously let go of rational thinking in order to discover the gold mine that lies deep within yourself.

Rational thought has its place, but it can never reveal the hidden treasures God has planted in the depths of your spirit. The inner man speaks a different language - the language of stillness, surrender, and inspired imagination. To reach the gold mine within, you must consciously release the need to control every thought, every answer, every outcome. Let the noise settle. Let the striving cease. When the natural mind grows quiet, the Spirit rises with clarity, whispering truths that cannot be reasoned out but must be revealed. It's in that sacred place where you begin to see with God's eyes. Ideas flow like streams in the desert. Insight comes as naturally as breathing. Creativity blossoms not from effort, but from communion with God, from allowing the divine life inside you to express itself without hindrance. The Creator lives in you, and His creativity longs to be released. Loosen your grip on logic and lean into His inspiration. Let go and let the Spirit paint upon the canvas of your soul.

Albert Einstein said, "I never made one of my discoveries through the process of rational thinking." He also said, "Creativity is intelligence having fun." Let your creative and imaginative mind run freely. It will take you places you never dreamed of and provide breakthroughs that others thought were impossible. What keeps life fascinating is the constant creativity of the soul. Let your thoughts lift you into creativity that is not hampered by the opinions of others. Bring your creativity to every encounter you have. Always remember that you were created creative and can invent new scenarios as frequently as they are needed. Channel your creativity into making the world a better place. Professor Brene Brown said,

"Creativity is the way I share my soul with the world." Be like Miles Davis who said, "My future starts when I wake up every morning. Every day I find something creative to do with my life." Writer Madeleine L'Engle said, "Unless we are creators we are not fully alive."

Creativity is a gift from God given for a specific purpose. When God has some work He wants done, He gives certain people the special ability to complete the task. To help you be great, God will give you creative abilities. In the Old Testament, a man named Bezalel was in charge of building the Tabernacle and the Ark of the Covenant. God said in Ex. 31:3, "And I have filled him with the Spirit of God, in wisdom, in understanding, in knowledge, and in all manner of workmanship." The skillfulness of Bezalel was creative artistry. He was gifted with the ability to bring together multiple materials and colors to create beautiful art for the Tabernacle. Bezalel was the first person in the Bible said to be "filled with the Spirit of God." This honor was given to him because he used his creativity to honor God. Notice he wasn't a preacher or a worship leader or a Bible teacher. No, he was a construction worker, an average guy who used his creative skills to bring glory to God.

Creativity is a way of living life no matter your vocation or how you earn a living. Being a creator is who God is. It's His nature to be creative. He then makes man and invites him to be creative just like He is. Every man has been given by God supernatural creativity. When you use your creativity it becomes the point of contact for miracles. God is the master creator and was creative in how He made the universe. Since we're made in His image, we have creativity birthed right into us as well. In other words, God created us to be creative. The first job God gave Adam was to name all the animals. He called Adam to think creatively. The spiritual gift of creativity is the special ability to spread the awareness of God's glory by creating things and new ways of doing things. Our creativity is a reflection of God as the ultimate creator. When you create something out of nothing but your imagination, you'll learn how great you are.

Creativity comes from God because He is the creator. We all have creativity within us. Your gifts and abilities are a reflection of the creativity of God. God has blessed every man with a creative imagination which encompasses the ability to discover new and original ideas, connections, and solutions to problems. As you grow in the Lord and become more spiritual, the more creative you will be. Your spirituality and creativity are so closely interconnected they are in effect one and the same. Creativity is defined as "the tendency to generate or recognize ideas, alternatives, or possibilities that may be useful in solving problems and communicating with others." Creativity opens the mind. It allows you to view and solve problems more openly, to find solutions that have a significant value and make a positive impact. Men who are great master their creativity. They visualize and create their own futures. They unleash their creativity as they verbalize what success means to them.

The world needs your creative ideas. They need your greatness to shine forth by inventing new ways to help make their lives better. Be creative. Help people see new ways of doing things instead of the common, mundane practices the world is throwing at them. Creativity is so important to the greatness of a man. The Father invented it, the Son modeled it, the Holy Spirit empowers it, and people need it. God is a glorious God and a part of His glory is His creativity. He created you in His image which means you are, in reality, a creative genius. Every day you have the opportunity to tap into the resurrection power of God that will give you the creativity to influence those around you. Creativity is when you turn "what if" into "what is." It's transcendent, it extends above and beyond the limits of ordinary everyday experiences. Creativity solves problems in a unique way. From deep within your inner man God will give you solutions you've never seen before. That's supernatural creativity.

Creativity is unlearned. Without ever reading a book children can come up with the most imaginative and created ideas the world has ever seen. To be great you must be creative in every area of your life. Greatness is never an accident. It is the fruit of a heart that listens to the whispers of the Spirit and dares to step beyond the limits of the ordinary. God did not create you to simply repeat what has already been done - He formed you in His own image, which means creativity is woven into the very fabric of your being. Creativity is not just for artists or musicians; it is for anyone who desires to live a life of purpose. It is the ability to see possibilities where others see problems, to find solutions where others feel stuck, to bring light into places that seem dim. When you allow God to breathe fresh ideas into you, you begin to walk in the kind of greatness that reflects His glory. Every area of life becomes a canvas where

God can paint something new, something beautiful, something powerful through you.

Be creative in your walk with God and in your prayer life and in how and when you read the Word. Be creative in how you seek Him. In your relationships, be creative in how you love. In your work, be creative in how you serve. In your challenges, be creative in how you rise above them. Let His creativity flow through your mind, your words, your decisions, and your actions. And as you do, your life will become a testimony of what God can do with a person who dares to dream with Him for in creativity, you discover the greatness God placed in you from the beginning. The better you know God, the more you'll do things in new and exciting ways. There's a spark in how you praise Him and how you relate to other people. You'll walk in creativity as you look at life from a different perspective. You'll see as God sees and with creativity you'll do the things God does. You'll look outside the box of normality and new thoughts and ideas will come to you as you set out to make this world a better place.

In order to release the creativity that is inside you, there must be order in your life. You must take time to seek God's input and divine direction. God's creativity is manifested in the world through great men who are a reflection of His creativity. It is God who tells you what needs to be done so listen to Him. Becoming creative won't happen on its own. You must be intentional in your quest to be creative. You must do the things that cause creativity to come. Questions emerge from creativity. Get curious and be eager to learn how to be creative. Ask questions of God and of those you see God using in a creative way. When you ask the right people the right questions, you'll get the right answers. Then go out and imitate their creativity as they imitate God's creativity. It is very important that you associate with the right people. You are to take what they do and channel it through your own creativity and make it your own for the number one secret of creativity is originality.

Albert Einstein said, "Creativity is seeing what others see and thinking what no one else ever thought." Read about creativity. Study it and meditate on it. Take naps in the afternoon with a pen and paper by your side. New ideas will come to you when your mind is the most rested. Get in the habit of taking walks by yourself. As you clear your mind of the hustle and bustle of life, new and creative ideas will come to you. It is your responsibility to carry God's creativity into the world. Don't ask Him to give you creativity, ask Him to release the creativity that is already there. Being creative brings God on the scene. Yes, He shows up when you're creative. You were created to be creative because all problems need a creative solution. Creativity is not a gimmick, it's a lifestyle. It's being open to the leading of the Holy Spirit. It's when God uses you to show the world His creativity. You are God's evidence to the world that He is still creating, still inspiring, still shaping lives with purpose and glory.

Every idea that stirs in your spirit, every gift that rises in your heart, every act of compassion, excellence, or faithfulness are the brushstrokes of God's creativity flowing through you. He uses your voice to speak colors into dark places. He uses your hands to build what only Heaven could imagine. He uses your life to display the depth, brilliance, and beauty of who He is. What is ultimately required in creativity is hard work, passion, faithfulness, and a commitment to excellence. It's when you want to serve God with everything you've got. Eccl. 9:10 says, "Whatever your hand finds to do, do it with all your might." A lazy person will never be creative. He'll never use the gifts and abilities God gave him. Your creativity is a gift from God that allows you to see life as God intends it to be. You use this gift so that the will of God will be done on earth as it is in heaven. When your creativity is being inspired by the Holy Spirit, you'll go into the world and create something beautiful, edifying, and enjoyable.

Creativity gives shape and substance to the heart of God. People can see God's creativity in the words and actions of His followers; in the things they say and do. The Hebrew word "bara" means 'to shape, fashion, create.' Creativity is cultivating wise thoughts, prudent words, and skillful actions to carry out God's will. Creativity is when you apply what you already know in a different way. The creative person thinks of ways to improve results and produce excellent work. A creative person will look for alternate routes when he comes to what appears to be a dead end. Creativity helps you find a way when there seems to be no way. What is creativity? It's the ability to look at something as it is, to see it for what it can be, and then doing the work to make it happen. It's the art of innovation and application. It's the art of solving problems in a new and unique way, in ways people have never thought of before. Creativity is your heritage and your nature. It's not something you wait on; it's something you stir up from within yourself.

God is saying, "You've got creativity, now use it!' He wants you to unleash the kind of creativity that He desires you to walk in. He wants you to ride on the crest of creativity. Creativity and stewardship go hand in hand. Ideas and innovation that are not acted upon forfeit their God-given authority to influence the world around you. Every creative act is a connection with God and His divine nature. Only good things come out of your union with God because when you're around someone perfect the standard goes up. It is God's nature to finish what He begins. The same nature that gives you creativity gives you the grace and the power to fulfill your destiny, to finish which you begin. Creativity is a process. It is intentional and it does not happen overnight. When you understand the value of your creativity you'll take the time needed to develop it. Creativity should be a high priority in your life because it is a huge part of your witness to the world. It's how you let your light shine before others. It's how you let people see how great you are.

| 9 |

"FAITHFUL STEWARDS"

To be great, you must be responsible. This truth is woven deeply into the fabric of our existence, for responsibility is not merely a task we perform - it is a sacred calling we embrace. God designed every soul with purpose, and with purpose comes the divine weight of stewardship. We are entrusted with our choices, our words, our relationships, and the gifts He has placed within us. Responsibility is the soil in which greatness grows. It teaches us discipline, shapes our character, and draws out the best that God has planted inside us. When we take ownership of our actions instead of excusing them, when we show up faithfully even when no one is watching, when we treat our commitments as holy assignments - we align ourselves with Heaven's design. The spiritually mature understand that responsibility is not a burden but a bridge. It links who we are today with who God is shaping us to become. It lifts us from potential to purpose, from calling to fulfillment.

In God's kingdom, greatness is never found in comfort or convenience, but in the faithful stewardship of the life He has entrusted to you. The first thing God gave Adam after He breathed life into him was responsibility. Gen. 2:15 says, "Then the Lord God took the man and put him in the garden of Eden to tend and keep it." That's responsibility. Next, He gave Adam the responsibility to name all the animals (vs. 19). Before God gave the human race the Ten Commandments and other moral laws to obey and follow, He first gave man responsibility. Responsibility was introduced to the world way back in Gen. 1:28. He told Adam and Eve to "be fruitful and multiply, fill the earth and subdue it." He then told them to "have dominion over the fish of the sea, over the birds of the air, and over every living thing that moves on the earth." In the beginning, God gave Adam and Eve responsibility. They were to rule over the earth, subdue it, and take care of all God's creation. Likewise, you were created to be responsible.

You will become great and be the most fulfilled and the most happy when there is something you are responsible for and you do it with all your heart and soul. Your ability and willingness to discipline yourself, to accept personal responsibility for your life, is essential to your happiness, health, success, and achievement. Without taking responsibility for your life, you will never be great. Accepting responsibility is one of the hardest of all disciplines but without it no success is possible. Responsibility is the great developer. It builds your character. It helps you grow. If you want to be great and do great things, be a man who takes responsibility. Taking responsibility is the fuel that sets your greatness ablaze. It's one of the most liberating, powerful, freedom-giving and opportunity-making character traits a man can have. Great men take responsibility for their future. Les Brown said, "If you take responsibility for yourself, you will develop a hunger to accomplish your dreams."

Responsibility is not a burden - it is a doorway. It is the moment you stop waiting for someone else to change your circumstances and start partnering with God to shape your destiny. When you take responsibility for your thoughts, your choices, your attitude, and your spiritual growth, something powerful awakens inside of you: hunger. This is a holy hunger, a hunger for the life God intended, a hunger for the dreams He whispered into your spirit long before you took your first breath. Responsibility aligns your heart with heaven. It shifts you from passive living to purposeful living. It opens your eyes to the truth that your dreams aren't accidental - they are seeds God planted within you. The moment you say, "Lord, I'll do my part," the fire ignites. You find yourself longing to learn more, to grow more, to rise higher. You begin to see obstacles not as barriers but as stepping-stones. You start walking with clarity, persistence, and faith because you know God moves through those who steward their own lives.

Responsibility is the price of freedom and success. Successful people have a social responsibility to make the world a better place and not just take from it. Your life begins to change the day you take responsibility for it. A great life awaits you if you'll accept the responsibility of consciously creating the future you want. Dalai Lama said, "Each of us must learn to work not just for his or her own self but for the benefit of all mankind. Universal responsibility is the real key to human survival." Everyone has been made for responsibility. God has given every man a destiny to fulfill and we must be faithful to do what He has called us to do. Do something worthwhile with your life. Without taking action, it's impossible to take responsibility. Move forward and your life will never be the same. The world grows brighter every time a man of God steps forward with integrity, compassion, and courage. Be a man who chooses righteousness over convenience, service over selfishness, and truth over compromise.

Gal. 6:5 says, "For each one shall bear his own load." You bear your own load by taking responsibility for your actions and expecting to be held accountable for them. In these few words lies a profound truth about spiritual maturity and personal responsibility. God has placed within every believer a unique calling, a divine assignment that no one else can carry out. While we are called to love one another, support one another, and lift the fallen, there remains a sacred portion of the journey that only you can walk. Your "load" is not a burden meant to crush you - it is the weight that strengthens your spiritual muscles. It is the part of your destiny God entrusts to you alone. No one can believe God for you. No one can obey God for you. No one can cultivate your prayer life, your faith, or your character on your behalf. These are the personal responsibilities that shape you into the image of Christ. When you willingly shoulder your God-given load, you honor the One who equipped you for the task.

You discover that the load you carry becomes the very tool God uses to deepen your faith and enlarge your endurance.

As you bear your load faithfully, you become stronger, wiser, and more sensitive to His voice. This scripture calls you to rise each day with a heart determined to make this world a better place, empowered by the Spirit of God and guided by the love of Christ. Embrace your assignment. Steward your walk with God. Lean into His grace. Responsibility means having the authority to pursue a given outcome and being accountable for that outcome. Like the sign said on the desk of Harry Truman, "The buck stops here." To be responsibility you must consider the consequences of your actions before proceeding and consider the consequences of your words before saying them. Refuse to blame others when things go wrong. Admit your mistakes, correct them, and learn from the experience. Don't let anything stop you from going forward.

Walk in integrity and keep your promises. Do what you say you will do. Be dependable. Be on time, pull your own weight, do the job right the first time. Be honest with people even when the truth hurts. Have the courage to say and do the right thing in all situations even when you don't benefit from doing so. Responsibility leaves no room for excuses, finger-pointing, or avoidance. If you don't carry your own load, then someone else will have to. Great men always carry their own load and are never a burden to others. To be responsible means to be trustworthy, to be reliable and dependable. It means you are a man who has the character to be honest and truthful. You can depend on a responsible man, a man who is loyal and dependable. He has the ability to carry out the assignment God placed on his life; thus he is great. A responsible man is accountable for he is able to justify his actions and decisions. He takes ownership of what happens as a result of the things he does and says.

A man of character, a man who can be counted on, is a man who can be trusted to act with integrity, make thoughtful decisions, and honor his commitments. He faces challenges with steadiness, prioritizes the well-being of those around him, and consistently follows through on his promises. Reliable and conscientious, he balances his own needs with the needs of others, taking accountability for his actions without deflecting blame. His maturity and foresight inspire confidence and respect, making him a dependable presence in both personal and professional spheres. He is a man who is led by the Spirit of God and is convinced that what he is doing is right and refuses to change what he believes or give it up. He is steadfast and constant in what he does and is very faithful, loyal, and resolute. He is firm in his allegiance to God and is unwavering in his convictions of what his assignment is. He recognizes that everything he has and everything he is comes as a gift from God.

In the Bible, a steward was the manager of the household. He was not the owner of the asset but was rather the responsible administrator of the owner's property. 1 Peter 4:10 says, "Each of you should use whatever gift you have received to serve others, as faithful stewards of God's grace in its various forms." The word "responsibility" is the ability to return to the original source what they gave you after you've fulfilled what they commissioned you to do. In simple terms, responsibility is the ability to respond. God has given you an assignment and you are to respond favorably to what He has told you to do. Notice the word "responsibility" is made up of three parts: re-spons-ibility. It means to 'return to the sponsor with all the ability He hid inside of you.' The parable of the talents teaches us you never return to the master only what he gave you. The servant who did that was cursed and called 'wicked and lazy.' Instead, God wants you to be responsible and return back to Him an increase on what He gave you.

It's your responsibility to bring increase to the kingdom of God. He wants your talent to come back bigger, better, fuller, and more fruitful. If He gives you a seed, it is your responsibility to return to Him a tree and later on a full-grown forest. There is nothing as destructive as irresponsibility, when you don't answer or submit to authority, when you lack a sense of accountability and don't respond to what your conscience is telling you. It means you are fickle. You're changing frequently, especially in regard to your loyalties, interests, and affections. You change your mind so much you can't be relied on. A person who is irresponsible is thoughtless, rash, and very unstable. They're always passing the blame onto someone else for the wrong actions and decisions they've made. They blame the past for their future, their parents for their habits, their teachers for their ignorance, their children for their social problems. They blame everybody but themselves.

You become irresponsible when you think life owes you something instead of you owing something to life. You have become ignorant of your accountability to help make this world a better place. If you mismanage something like that wicked and lazy servant, God will take it from you. A lot of things people think the devil took from them was in fact taken by God. To be great you must appreciate the gifts and talents and abilities God has given you, along with the capacity to carry out His will and fulfill your destiny. He put a great treasure inside of you. He's given you strength and wisdom and potential and He is now demanding a "response ability" from you. He is demanding that He receives this treasure back with increase. To be great you must manifest your ability to respond to this demand that is being placed upon you. The principle is clear: God gives, and He expects multiplication. He is demanding that what He has placed in your hands be returned to Him with increase.

In the wilderness God provided the needs of the people. He gave them water from a rock, rained bread down from heaven, sent quail for them to eat. But it was different in the Promised Land. In the land flowing with milk and honey they had to dig their own wells, grow their own food, breed their own cattle. They had to protect their own territory, sew their own clothes, and take care of their own families. Why did this happen? Because God demanded responsibility from the people. You must take responsibility to read the Word daily, to "set your mind on things above, not on things on the earth" (Col. 3:2). The Message Bible says, "Look up, and be alert to what is going on around Christ. That's where the action is. See things from His perspective." Men who are great are responsible for their own spiritual growth. With maturity comes the responsibility to fight your own battles. God will fight with you; He won't fight for you. Be strong and courageous and you will come out victorious."

You need to be responsible for all the things God has given you. Be responsible to pay your bills, to walk in integrity, to love, nurture, and protect your family. Matt. 22:14 says, "Many are called, but few are chosen." Jesus is saying that many are called but few are willing to take the responsibility for the call. Everything you get, every privilege God gives you, comes with a corresponding responsibility. The problem is people ask God for big things but don't want the responsibility that goes with it. People want a big house but they don't want the responsibility to pay the huge mortgage bill, to clean it, to fix the things that are sure to break down. Consider the children of Israel who died in the wilderness because they didn't want the responsibility of driving out the giants who lived in the Promised Land. Taking responsibility gives a person power over themselves and provides positive energy and spiritual strength to achieve their God-given potential.

You must take responsibility because life is a fight and not a lazy float down the river of blessing. In order to take responsibility, you must have courage. Courage is defined as "the state or quality of mind or spirit that enables one to face danger, fear, change, or uncertainty with confidence, resolution, and bravery." Taking responsibility for your life means you'll do what's right no matter what, that you'll rise above the difficulties forced upon you that try to slow you down. Taking responsibility is about keeping your eyes focused on God at all times as you continually go in the right direction in spite of what is taking place around you. Eph. 5:15 (JBP), "Live life, then, with a due sense of responsibility, not as men who do not know the purpose of life but as those who do." The Passion Translation says in vs. 16, "Live honorably with true wisdom, for we are living in evil times. Take full advantage of every day as you spend your life for His purposes."

Make the best use of your time, despite all the difficulties of these days. Don't be vague but firmly grasp what you know to be the will of God. Men who are great conduct themselves with integrity and always demonstrate a strong sense of responsibility. They leave a legacy of honesty, love, and peace. Men who are responsible stand tall with their chin up and shoulders back. They live without shame as they display a noble, uncorrupted life. Taking responsibility is the willingness to give account for your actions, the willingness to bear the burden of what you have or have not done. A responsible man is one who can be counted on, a man who is trustworthy and reliable. He is the type of man God can use to further His kingdom. God has given you dominion over your life and He wants you to do something with it. You are a steward of the things of God and He wants a return on His investment. He wants you to take action, to develop the maturity to lay your own will aside as you strive to fulfill His will.

You are responsible for your own success in life and ministry. God does not make your choices for you. If you ask, He'll tell you what to do but ultimately the choice is yours. Be responsible for your life. Live with integrity and honesty. Be truthful in your words and actions. Keep your promises and live a life that is free from deception and dishonesty. Responsibility is the foundation on what all eternal values are built on. Greatness comes when you personally accept responsibility for your choices, your character, and your morals. Why live responsibly? Because God is watching your life (Heb. 4;13). God made an investment in you, and He expects a return on His investment. Daniel Webster once said, "The most important idea I ever thought was the day I realized that I am personally and individually accountable to God for how I lived." God expects all men to be responsible, to make sacrifices for the good of others. It's what a spouse looks for, what children need, what makes a strong society and nation.

If you want to do all that God has called you to do so that He gets all the glory, then it starts with you taking responsibility for your life. The time is now to man up and stop blaming your spouse, your parents, your teachers, or the lack of opportunities for who you are and who you are becoming. Look in the mirror and say, "The buck stops here." The Bible says, "We are more than conquerors through Christ" (Rom. 8:37). This doesn't leave much room for excuses. God has a great plan for your future so stop making excuses as to why or how you can't get there. Take responsibility for who you are and who you want to become. Men who are great take responsibility and trust God to provide them with everything they need to become the person He is calling them to be. By taking responsibility for who you are today, you open the door for transformation, allowing His Spirit to guide you toward who you are meant to become. Trust that the journey of personal responsibility is also a journey of divine partnership.

| 10 |

"WISDOM FROM ABOVE"

The Bible makes it very clear that true greatness is never measured by power, wealth, or status but by wisdom. To walk in greatness, you must first walk in wisdom - choosing the path of discernment, patience, and humility. Prov. 4:7 says, "Wisdom is the principle thing; therefore, get wisdom." The NLT says, "Getting wisdom is the wisest thing you can do." The CSB says, "Wisdom is supreme so get wisdom! And whatever else you get, get understanding." The MSG says, "Never walk away from wisdom - she guards your life. Love her - she keeps her eye on you. Above all and before all, do this: Get wisdom!" Greatness without wisdom is like a house built on sand - it may rise high, but it will fall in the storms of life. True greatness, however, is grounded in the fear of the Lord, in understanding His ways, and in applying His Word to every decision. When you seek wisdom, you align your hearts with God's will, influence others positively, and leave a legacy that honors Him.

To be great you must be passionate in your pursuit of wisdom. No price is too high for wisdom. Give everything you've got to get it. Getting wisdom is not a one-time event. It is not obtained in a moment but progressively over the duration of a person's life. The attainment of wisdom is a matter of desire and will. God does not give His children the taste of His delights until they begin to sweat in seeking after them. Wisdom involves seeing life from God's perspective and acting accordingly. With wisdom you'll know what the consequences will be tomorrow for the decisions you make today. To walk in wisdom you must remove the shackles of earthbound thinking and commit to seeing life through the eyes of God. Men who are great live to glorify God. They pray, "Lord, help me to see this situation from Your perspective and make right choices that please You." Prov. 3:5,6 warns us not to lean on our own understanding but to trust the One who knows all things, the One who knows the end from the beginning.

The Bible makes it clear that wisdom is more than knowledge - it is a way of life that unlocks God's blessings. When we choose to walk in wisdom, we align ourselves with God's principles, and His promises begin to unfold in our lives. Scripture teaches that wisdom brings life in abundance: it guides our steps, protects our hearts, and opens doors to every good thing. Long life, prosperity, and health are not mere coincidences but are natural companions of a life lived wisely. As you seek understanding, make decisions grounded in God's truth, and honor Him in all you do, you set the stage for His blessings to follow. Wisdom will take you beyond the way things look to the way they really are. It takes you beyond how you feel and causes you to do what is right. Wisdom is the eye that directs the foot of obedience. Those who walk in wisdom are the saints of God. They are His portion and the lot of His inheritance (Deut. 32:9). God's gift of wisdom will literally change your life.

Daniel prayed, "To You, O God of my fathers, I give thinks and praise for You have given me wisdom and power" (Dan. 2:23). Wisdom is indispensable to a man of God. It leads to higher worship, greater faith, deeper holiness, and better service to the King of kings and Lord of lords. No wonder Prov. 16;16 says, "How much better to get wisdom than gold! To get understanding is to be chosen rather than silver." Yes, wisdom is worth more than all the money in the world. No one is born wise. You must acquire wisdom from God if you are to be truly wise. Prov. 2:6 says, "For the Lord gives wisdom; From His mouth come knowledge and understanding." Knowledge, understanding, and wisdom go together but they are not the same. Knowledge is information, understanding is comprehension, and wisdom is application. Dan. 12:4 tells us in the last days people will be running to and fro searching for knowledge. That definitely describes the world we are living in today.

All the knowledge in the world won't do you any good if you can't comprehend it and if you don't apply it properly. Wisdom is a valuable thing. Prov. 8:11 says, "For wisdom is better than rubies, and all the things one may desire cannot be compared with her." Godly wisdom is from God and honors God. Prov. 9:10 says, "The fear of the Lord is the beginning of wisdom, and the knowledge of the Holy One is understanding." Godly wisdom starts with a holy reverence for God and results in a holy life. We recognize we are citizens of another kingdom and make right choices accordingly. Godly wisdom is not merely knowledge or cleverness - it begins in the heart with a deep, holy reverence for the Lord. When you honor God above all, acknowledging His sovereignty and seeking His guidance, your heart gets aligned with His truth. This reverence transforms your thoughts, words, and actions, guiding you to live a life that reflects His holiness.

A life rooted in holy reverence inevitably becomes a holy life, marked by integrity, compassion, and righteousness. Walking in godly wisdom is a journey of the heart: it starts with awe for God and leads to a life set apart for His glory. James 3:13 (NLT) says, "If you are wise and understand God's ways, prove it by living an honorable life, doing good works with the humility that comes from wisdom." James is saying you can look at a person's life and determine if what they're saying is based on worldly wisdom or wisdom from above. A truly wise person is known by the way they live their life. The MSG says, "Live well, live wisely, live humbly. It's the way you live, not the way you talk, that counts." Wisdom is a lifestyle. A man can be very smart but if he's not a person of godly character and integrity all that knowledge won't do him any good. You show by good conduct that you are a person of wisdom. The Greek word for "good" means 'beautiful' and 'well pleasing.'

James is saying that a wise man lives a beautiful life, a life marked by doing good deeds, a life that is well pleasing to God. Don't be like Solomon who was a very smart man but confusion and disorder were the mark of his many fractured relationships showing us that brilliance without spiritual alignment can still lead to brokenness. Solomon was known for his great wisdom, yet his life reminds us that intelligence alone does not guarantee peace, clarity, or fulfillment. His mind could solve complex problems, but his heart often followed desire without restraint. To be great you must do what Jesus said in Matt. 10:16, "Be wise as serpents." Yes, a serpent is very wise and has keen eyesight and is quick to learn. With the serpent's eye you'll have quick insight into the truths of God's Word. With the eye of the serpent you'll gain wisdom and will be divinely illuminated. The word "wise" is the Greek word "pronimos" which means 'prudent, careful, cunning, discerning, thoughtful, intelligent, sensible.'

These words perfectly depict the behavior and actions of snakes. Serpents have a way of blending into the environment when they move into a new territory. They don't announce their presence but lay low and stay quiet. If a new door of opportunity is being opened for you, it is a wise thing to move slowly and carefully. Take the time to gather all the facts before a decision is made. Lay low, stay quiet, and blend into the environment. Moving too fast may cause you to make poor decisions you'll greatly regret farther down the road. Moving slowly may take more time but in the end it will produce more stable and lasting results. The snake knows when to be still and when to strike and take action. Timing is everything. It's the key to fulfilling any assignment God has given you. For the serpent, this knowledge is the key to its survival. If its prey passes before him and the snake waits too long to strike, he'll miss the opportunity put before him and he'll go hungry.

True wisdom always comes from above. Ancient Jewish writers have described wisdom as "the breath of the power of God, a pure influence flowing from the glory of the Almighty." The top priority of wisdom is that it must be pure, it must be undefiled by sin. God is holy and pure and so is the wisdom that comes from Him. James 3:17, "But the wisdom that is from above is first pure, then peaceable, gentle, willing to yield, full of mercy, and good fruit, without partiality, and without hypocrisy." God is holy and pure, and His nature is without blemish, untouched by the imperfections of this world. The wisdom that flows from Him mirrors this divine perfection - it is untainted, righteous, and life-giving. When you seek God's guidance, you are not merely receiving knowledge; you are connecting with a sacred source that illuminates truth, brings clarity to confusion, and aligns your heart with His purposes. Just as His holiness calls us to reverence, His wisdom calls us to obedience and discernment.

Embrace the pure and eternal wisdom of God, allowing it to shape your thoughts, words, and actions for His glory. There is no pride, jealousy, or selfish ambition in wisdom that comes from above. It is sweeter than honey to the taste. It brings people closer to God and one another. Man's wisdom leads to rivalry and war (James 4:1) but God's wisdom leads to peace. It desires peace, promotes peace, seeks peace. James says wisdom is also gentle. To be gentle means to be "kind-hearted, sweet-spirited, self-controlled" (AMP). It's wisdom that brings people closer together. The word "gentle" comes from the Greek word that describes a wild horse that has been tamed. Its strength is under control and ready to be used by its master. Those who are gentle are the strongest and wisest people on the planet. They don't over-react and are not driven by their emotions. 1 Cor. 4;13 (NLT) says, "We respond gently when evil things are said about us." That's strength under control. That's the gentleness of wisdom from above.

Gentleness is very persuasive. Prov. 25;15 (NCV) says, "A gentle word can get through to the hard-headed." The CEV says, "Patience and gentle talk can overcome any problem." In a noisy and impatient world, God has given His people a different kind of strength - one that does not shout, does not rush, and does not force its way through life. It is the strength of patience and the healing touch of gentle talk. These two virtues carry a spiritual power that can overcome barriers no argument or anger ever could. Prov. 15:1 says, "A gentle answer turns away wrath, but a harsh word stirs up anger." When you choose gentleness over retaliation, you are choosing the very character of Christ. He conquered hearts not through force, but through a soft voice, compassionate eyes, and a patient spirit that waited for people to turn toward truth. Patience is not weakness - it is spiritual confidence. It says, "I trust God's timing more than my own frustration."

Patience is the quiet assurance that the Holy Spirit is working even when nothing seems to be changing. When you remain patient, you are standing on a higher foundation, refusing to let circumstances dictate your peace. And when patience meets gentle talk, miracles happen. Hard hearts begin to soften. Tense atmospheres begin to shift. Arguments lose their fire. Barriers of misunderstanding begin to crumble. Gentle talk carries the fragrance of Christ - it speaks life where the world speaks accusation. Every problem you face today - whether in your home, your workplace, your relationships, or even within yourself - can be transformed by these two divine tools. You don't have to overpower anything. Let your calm spirit be your weapon. Let your kind words be your strategy. Let your patience be your testimony. When you slow down and speak with the grace God has given you, you invite His presence into the situation. And wherever His presence enters, peace follows, problems shift, and hearts are healed.

Walk in patience. Speak with gentleness. And watch God turn impossible moments into powerful testimonies of His love and wisdom working through you. The wiser you are, the more pleasant you will be. And the more pleasant you are, the more persuasive you will become. Prov. 16:21 (TEV) says, "A wise, mature person is known for understanding. The more pleasant his words, the more persuasive he is." God designed the human heart to respond to kindness, gentleness, and grace. These qualities carry a divine fragrance that people instinctively recognize, even if they cannot explain it. A pleasant spirit is the overflow of a heart touched by God. When the Holy Spirit is allowed to shape our inner life, He produces a sweetness that makes our presence comforting, our words trustworthy, and our influence meaningful. Pleasantness is not weakness; it is Christlikeness. When you carry peace within, you create peace around you.

When your words are seasoned with grace, they open doors that arguments never could. People listen differently when they feel valued. They open their hearts when they do not feel attacked. They are moved when they sense genuine love behind your words. The world is loud, harsh, and hurried. That is why a pleasant spirit stands out so powerfully. It is a lamp in a dark place, a calming breeze in a storm. Pleasantness disarms resistance and draws people toward truth - not by pressure, but by presence. If you want to be more persuasive in your conversations, your ministry, your leadership, or even your relationships, begin by cultivating the fruit of the Spirit within. Let Christ's gentleness shape your tone, let His kindness influence your responses, and let His peace govern your reactions. For when your spirit is pleasant, your life becomes a message and people will want to hear every word. You don't have to strive to be noticed; God Himself makes your life a testimony.

When the heart is at peace with God, the soul shines with a quiet radiance that draws people near. The best way to improve any relationship is to speak in a gentle voice. Ruth said to Boaz, "You are very kind to me. You have made me feel better by speaking gently to me" (Ruth 2:13). James also says wisdom is willing to yield. The ESV says it is "open to reason." It means to be teachable and willing to listen. Get rid of pride that says you're always right. Next, James says wisdom from above is full of mercy and good fruits. Mercy is compassion that leads to action. It is forever ready to help those who are hurting. A man's actions can reveal if the words he speaks is wisdom from God. If he is loving and considerate, then what he says in humility originated in the throne of God. True wisdom is without partiality. It does not create division and discord. It has no hidden motives. It doesn't speak for the purpose of getting something from someone else. It is constant and unwavering, not hot one day and cold the next.

Wisdom from above is very sincere and without hypocrisy. It doesn't wear a mask for it is straight forward and genuine. Finally, James says one of the primary traits of those who have godly wisdom is they are peacemakers (James 3:18). They treat everyone with dignity and honor. Since wisdom plays such a prominent part in a man's greatness, it is a vital necessity to know how to get this wisdom from above. The primary way to get wisdom is by learning God's Word. Ps. 119:169 says "Give me understanding according to Your word." Ps. 119:98, "Your commands are always with me and make me wiser than my enemies. I have more insight than all my teachers for I meditate on Your statutes." You can also develop godly wisdom by fellow shipping with those who exhibit wisdom in their own lives. Ps.13:20, "Whoever walks with the wise becomes wise." The Bible also tells us when we need wisdom, we only need to ask God for it and He'll give it to us. But we must ask in faith with plans to obey.

James 1:5 says, "If any of you lacks wisdom, let him ask of God who gives to all liberally and without reproach, and it will be given to him." The Message Bible says, "If you don't know what you're doing, pray to the Father. He loves to help. Ask boldly, believingly, without a second thought." Pray and ask for wisdom. God wants you to have His wisdom. He is delighted to give it to you when your heart is ready to receive it. God is doing a powerful work on this earth in the midst of all this chaos and calamity. You'll need His wisdom if you're to join Him in the work He's doing. God is a giving God and He'll give you the wisdom you're asking for. Ask to see things from His perspective, to see His plan for your life. When you ask God for wisdom, you are asking for something that is already in His heart to give. That means you never have to fear that your questions are too big, too small, or too frequent. Not only does He give wisdom - He gives it generously.

Trials don't bring eternal blessings but being steadfast through them does. For that to happen, you'll need God's wisdom. The problem most people have is they ask for deliverance from the trial instead of the wisdom to help them endure what's going on. Nobody ever got stronger by having their problems taken away. No, you grow up spiritually by asking for God's wisdom that will give you the endurance to go through it. If you don't have this wisdom, ask for it. The NLT says, "He will not rebuke you for asking." God wants to generously give you wisdom, but He won't force it on you. You must ask for wisdom. You must seek and desire it with all your heart and soul. With that asking comes the assurance He'll give it to you (Rom. 8:32). God wants to bring you to the next level of spiritual maturity through the trial you're in. Asking for and receiving godly wisdom will result in you having joy in the midst of your trial. You rejoice because you know you'll be stronger when you come out on the other side.

People who struggle are not asking for God's wisdom. The word "ask" in Greek is a continual, purposeful action. It's the same word used in Matt. 7:7 where Jesus said, "Keep on asking, and you will receive what you ask for." You need to ask and keep asking God for His wisdom to bring you through life's trials with steadfastness and joy. Ask with focused intent and He'll give it to you. For sure, God is well pleased when you ask for His wisdom. Solomon asked for wisdom and an understanding heart and 1 Kings 3:10 says this request "pleased the Lord." God will give you His wisdom but not without your genuine faith. It's faith that brings God's wisdom into your life so you'll know what to do when the storms of life blow. James 1:6 says, "But let him ask in faith with no doubting, for he who doubts is like a wave of the sea driven and tossed by the wind." God will give you what you confidently expect Him to give. If you're going to receive God's wisdom, you must go to Him in faith that is genuine with no doubting.

To those who doubt, James 1:7,8 says, "For let not that man suppose that he will receive anything from the Lord, he is a double-minded man, unstable in all his ways." Don't allow negative circumstances to cause you to doubt the goodness of God or His willingness to give you the wisdom you need. How you respond in trials is what reveals the type of man you really are. Do you trust God or don't you? Are you great or are you not great? A life-changing opportunity comes every time you walk in faith and wisdom. During hard times you can have a perspective that far outweighs whatever you're going through. Men who are great obey the words of Col. 3:2, "Set your mind on things above, not things on the earth." This new perspective will cause you to see the unseen, and this is what faith is all about. You're clinging to Jesus, and you know everything is going to work out in your favor. You don't see what the world sees, you see what God sees. You've got the right perspective, and this is what will carry you to victory.

| 11 |

"A GREATNESS MULTIPLIED"

David said in Ps. 18:35, "You have also given me the shield of Your salvation; Your right hand has held me up, Your gentleness has made me great." When David wrote these words, he wasn't speaking as a man who had lived an easy life - he was speaking as a man who had survived life. He knew what it meant to be hunted, misunderstood, pressured, stretched, and overwhelmed. And yet, in all of it, he recognized one unshakable truth: God Himself had been his protection, his strength, and the One who lifted him higher than he could have ever climbed on his own. God doesn't merely give you a shield -He is the shield. His salvation surrounds you like armor. It guards your mind, your emotions, your calling, and your destiny. When the enemy throws accusations, doubts, fears, or temptations, the shield of the Lord absorbs the blow. You may feel the pressure, but it cannot penetrate what God Himself is covering.

The right hand in Scripture represents authority, power, and favor. God says, "I am not watching you from a distance -

I am holding you up." Your life is not being upheld by your discipline, your wisdom, or your endurance, but by the God who refuses to let you collapse under the weight of your battles. David, a warrior, attributes his greatness not to God's power but to God's gentleness. The Hebrew word for "gentleness" is "anvah" and can mean 'humility, meekness, and help.' However, it can also mean 'condescension.' In the Bible, the word "condescension" means 'to go or come down.' It is the willingness to lower oneself to another's level. Another translation says, "You have stooped down to make me great." This is incredible. God stooped down from His throne in heaven to make a shepherd boy the king of all Israel. This, also, is how you become great. In Christ, God has stooped down to your lowly world to pick you up and make you great in Him.

Yes, there is greatness inside of you waiting to be developed and released. We have been made kings and priests unto God (Rev. 1:6). Ps. 71:21 says, "You shall increase my greatness, and comfort me on every side." It is one thing to be great; it's another thing to have your greatness multiplied. God has stooped down in Christ to make you great for the unique purpose of advancing His kingdom here on the earth. The measure of your usefulness sets the height and width for your greatness, by the degree to which your life becomes an instrument in the hands of the Master. Just as a vessel is shaped according to the purpose it is meant to serve, your greatness takes form according to the measure of your usefulness in God's plan. This is why, no matter how great you are, He wants to increase your greatness. Your greatness isn't measured by how many people serve you, it's measured by how many people you serve. Greatness is found not in its size, but in its service.

Greatness expands when your willingness to serve expands. When your hands are open, your heart is tender, and your life is available, God increases your capacity. He stretches your height - lifting you into spiritual maturity - and widens your influence, allowing your life to touch more souls than you ever imagined. The world tells you to seek recognition. Heaven tells you to seek usefulness. The world demands that you prove yourself. God simply asks that you present yourself as a living sacrifice. There should never be any doubt that you are here on this planet to fulfill a divine purpose. To be great you must discover what that purpose is. The greatest discovery in your life will be the day you know and understand why you are here. This is important because your purpose distinguishes you from everybody else. If you don't know your purpose, life will have no true meaning for you. You'll run to and from like a chicken with its head cut off.

With no purpose life becomes one big experiment. You'll marry the first person who comes around, and you'll go from one job to another in search of fulfillment. For you, life will be a maze of confusion. You won't know if you're coming or going as you consistently waste your time, money, energy, and talents on things that have no meaning. Purpose changes all that. It releases you from the experiments of trying to figure out why you're here. On the contrary, it makes your life precise. Precision comes from purpose. If you know where you're going, you can be very precise in the decisions you make to get

there. Without purpose all you'll do is live a dull, boring existence. You'll do the same thing every day of your life. You'll get
up, go to work, come home, watch TV, go to bed. You'll get
paid far less than you're worth as you work endlessly to make
someone else rich. After forty years you'll retire and spend the
rest of your days in a rocking chair on your front porch.

Spiritual emptiness is a universal disease. People everywhere
say, "There's got to be more to life than this." There is more
to life and knowing your purpose helps you discover what that
is. There is no substitute for purpose. There is no satisfaction
without knowing who you are and why you're here. You will
only be great if you do what you were born to do. A lot of men
do good things but they're not doing the right things. They're
not doing what God told them to do. Fulfilling your purpose is
when you do the right thing. Before you were born there was
a purpose for your life. What this means is that your birth became necessary because of your destiny. Your purpose existed
before you were born and it is continually pulling you forward
in life. When you go off course your purpose will pull you back
onto the right path. Your destiny is calling out to you every
moment of every day. It silently screams at you to fulfill what
has already been established by God for your life.

No matter what you do or where you go, your purpose will
be there speaking in your ear. You can try to outrun it, bury it
beneath distractions, or drown it in busyness, but purpose is
not something you choose - it's something God has woven into
the very fabric of your being. It is the whisper in your ear in
the quiet moments, the tug in your spirit when you feel unset-

tled, the holy restlessness that rises whenever you stray from the path He designed for you. You cannot hide from what God has ordained. You cannot silence the calling He placed within you before you ever took your first breath. Purpose will wait for you. Purpose will pursue you. Purpose will speak - softly at times, urgently at others - until you turn and face the very thing you were born to do. Even in seasons where you feel lost, your purpose is not lost. Even when you feel unworthy, God's calling over your life remains unchanged. And even if you take the long road, His purpose for you is still right there - steady, patient, and unshaken.

The truth be told, fulfilling your purpose is more important than the purpose itself. Why? Because most men are good beginners but very poor finishers. You must fulfill you destiny. You must finish what you begin. Luke 9:62 (NLT) says, "Anyone who puts his hand to the plow and then looks back is not fit for the kingdom of God." Once you put your hand to the plow of fulfilling your purpose and look back, you'll live a crooked life full of uncertainty. Plowing and purpose both require single-minded focus. It is of vital importance that you fulfill the calling on your life. This is how the mission gets accomplished and God's purpose gets fulfilled. What is purpose? It's the ultimate original reason for the creation of something. Your mission is the assignment you've been given to fulfill your purpose. It will help if you understand that once you gave your life to Christ your life is no longer your own. It belongs to God and it's now your responsibility to do what He wants you to do.

Eph. 2:10 says you were created to do good works which God planned before time began, works He prearranged and made ready for you to fulfill. Rejoice that you are not at the mercy of fate and circumstance. What's more, God has put inside you the gifts, talents, and potential to fulfill that which He has planned for you to do. Have confidence knowing that God is directing your steps each and every day. Have peace knowing God goes before you preparing the way you should go. God speaks in a still, small voice and He desires for you to lean in and rely upon His direction for your life as you grow in your relationship with Him. Trust God and He'll take you on a glorious journey that will take you to the fulfillment of your purpose. This journey will require from you perseverance and persistence. Perseverance is a continual effort to do or achieve something despite difficulties, failure, or opposition. It's the action of being steadfast and determined.

When you've done all you can do, pray and keep praying, ask and keep asking, knock and keep knocking, seek and keep seeking (Matt. 7:7,8). Someone who is persistent continues to do something even though it is difficult or other people come against them. They keep pressing forward and never give up. Your purpose in life should be something you take very, very seriously. Men who are great use all their energy and resources to serve God and His purposes. They're like Hezekiah who "did what was right in the sight of the Lord, according to all that his father David had done" (2 Kings 2:3). Vs. 5 says, "He trusted in the Lord God of Israel, so that after him was none like him among all the kings of Judah, nor any who were before him." Vs. 6, "For he held fast to the Lord; he did not depart from following Him, but kept His commandments, which the Lord had commanded Moses." Hezekiah knew that purpose is everything, that without purpose life has no meaning.

Without purpose you'll have no reason to get up in the morning. Paul understood this. He wrote, "Be careful how you live. Live wisely, not foolishly. Make the most of your time and take every opportunity to do good because evil is everywhere. Don't live carelessly without thinking. Instead, make sure you understand what the Lord wants you to do with your life" (Eph. 5:15-17). Be righteous and live a holy life. Paul told Timothy, "If you keep your life clean from sin, you will be an instrument that God can use for His highest purposes" (2 Tim. 2:21). To be an instrument that God can use is the highest desire of all men who are great. They're like Isaiah who said, "Here I am! Send me" (Is. 6:8). To be great, to be used by God, you must at all times center your life around Him. Greatness is not self-centered, it's God-centered. When God becomes the center of your life, everything else takes its rightful place. Your dreams align with His will. Your strength flows from His presence. Your value is rooted in His love.

God made you so that He could love you. To be great you must love Him the same way He loves you. In other words, you must make Him the center of your life. Jesus said, "Love the Lord your God with all your heart and soul and mind and strength. This is the first and greatest commandment" (Matt. 22:37,38). The first purpose of your life is to let God love you and to love Him back. Why? Because God made you to have a close and lasting relationship with Him. This is one way to worship God. Worship is more than singing and clapping your hands and stomping your feet. In simple terms, worship is enjoying God's love. Any time you put your focus on God, when you talk to Him and listen to Him, you are, in fact, worshiping Him. It's when you center your life on God. Anything that comes before God in your life is called an idol. Too many men put fortune and fame and social relationships before God and have made these things idols in their life.

How do you know if something besides God is at the center of your life? You'll start to worry and get stressed out, anxious, and unsettled. These are not just emotions - they are spiritual warning lights on the dashboard of your heart. They signal that something else has claimed the throne that belongs only to Him. Worry is often the first indicator that your focus has shifted from the Almighty to the uncertain. Stress reveals that your eyes are more on the problem than on the Provider. Anxiety whispers that you're leaning on your own strength instead of resting in His. In contrast to this, if God is the nucleus and most important part of your life, you'll have peace. You'll stop worrying because your faith is in Him. Phil. 4:7 says, "And the peace of God which surpasses all understanding, will guard your hearts and minds through Christ Jesus." When God is truly at the center of your life, there is a deep inner steadiness that no circumstance can shake. His peace becomes the anchor of your soul.

The second great purpose of your life is to love God's people, your fellow brothers and sisters in the Lord, those who call Jesus their Savior just like you do. Love is important to God because He is love (1 John 4:8). First, you love God with all your heart and soul and then you "love your neighbor as yourself" (Matt. 22:39). To be great you must love one another, help one another, serve one another, care for one another, comfort for one another, greet one another, and pray for one another. You love people by having fellowship with them. Heb. 10:25 (TEV) says, "Let us not give up the habit of meeting together." MSG, "Let's us see how inventive we can be in encouraging love and helping out." Living life as a man of God is not a solo act. In the heart of every person is a longing for belonging. We all need one another. We're not meant to face life alone. Scripture reveals that even the mightiest warriors were never meant to walk by themselves. David had Jonathan. Moses had Aaron. Paul had Timothy.

Next, God wants you to grow in Him, to cultivate spiritual maturity, to become like Jesus Christ. Heb. 6:1 (TLB) says, "Let us go on and become mature in our understanding, as strong Christians ought to be." This strength is not measured by worldly standards, but by faith, character, and the ability to live consistently according to God's truth. Just as a child must grow to become an adult, so must a believer progress from foundational teachings toward a fuller, richer experience of God. This third purpose is called "discipleship." Another word for "disciple" is "student." You're not spinning your wheels in the mud but are forever learning new things about God and His kingdom. We all grow old but not everyone grows up spiritually. They get stuck in perpetual immaturity. They're saved but they're shallow, thus they are not great. Maturity is not an end in itself, it's a tool for ministry. It helps you explain kingdom principles to others, to help others grow up and be mature also.

This leads to the fourth purpose for your life. God wants you to give and contribute something back into His kingdom. He wants you to be unselfish and to serve others. 1 Peter 4:10 (TLB) says, "God has given each of you some special abilities; be sure to use them to help each other." Greatness is based on what you do for those around you. The Message Bible says, "Be generous with the different things God gave you, passing them around so all get in on it: if words, let it be God's words; if help, let it be God's hearty help." This act of service is called "ministry." When you make a contribution with your life, when you help someone else in any way, you have ministered to them. God will use you in the areas that bring you the most joy. The passion you have for what you do will maximize the talents and abilities God gave you. If you want to be great in God's kingdom, learn to be the servant of all (Matt. 20:26). Jesus made it very clear that your significance, your greatness, is based on what you do for others.

Strive to be like David who asked, "What can I give back to God for the blessings He's poured out on me?" (Ps. 116:12 MSG). If you crave significance, then ask God this same question. Significance does not come from your status in the community or from financial success. It comes when God uses you to help make the lives of other people better. It's only when you give your life away that you'll really learn what it means to live. Jesus said in Matt. 16:25, "Whoever loses his life for My sake will find it." Only those who are great live unselfishly.

Dying to self and living for God and others is the only way to a happy and fulfilling life in this world and the world to come. Finally, the fifth purpose of your life is to tell others about the love God has for them. Pass on to those around you the same amazing love God has given you. Men who are great are ambassadors for Christ (2 Cor. 5:20). God has given each of us the task of telling everyone what He is doing on the earth.

The Message Bible says, "We're Christ's representatives. God uses us to persuade men and women to drop their differences and enter into God's work of making things right between them." The NCV says, "We have been sent to speak for Christ!" This is called "witnessing." You are here to be a witness to others of God's great, abundant, and everlasting love. An ambassador is both a messenger for and a representative of the one who sent him. Just as an ambassador lives in a foreign land, so also do the great men of God. Though citizens of heaven (Phil. 3:20), they represent their King in this evil and corrupt world where they live as aliens and strangers (1 Peter 2:11). They proclaim to the lost, perishing rebels of this fallen world the good news that they can be reconciled to the King of heaven (Rom. 10:13). It's the Holy Spirit who persuades people to accept Christ as their Lord and Savior (John 16:8). Your responsibility as a witness is to tell others what God has done for you.

| 12 |

"GOOD COMMUNICATION"

We are all here to make this world a better place. Your success in influencing other people to live a better life is all based on how well you communicate with them. Your ability to positively impact the lives of others is not measured by wealth, position, or authority - it is measured by the clarity, love, and wisdom with which you communicate. God has placed within each of us the responsibility to encourage, guide, and uplift others. Yet, this calling can only be fulfilled when we speak in a way that touches hearts and opens minds. Spiritual influence begins with listening, understanding, and then speaking truth in love. When your words are gentle yet powerful, rooted in wisdom and compassion, you become a vessel through which God can transform lives. Strive to speak not to impress, but to bless. Speak not to win arguments, but to awaken hearts. In doing so, you will not only influence lives - you will fulfill the higher calling God has placed on you as a messenger of hope, truth, and life.

To be great you must be able to share with others in a way that they'll understand what you're saying. Good communication makes you effective in a society that has lost its way. Communication is all about connecting with people. You must connect to their hearts as well as their minds. To be effective what you say must be clear and precise. Know the person you're talking to for not everybody will receive what you're saying the same way. There is no one-size-fits-all when it comes to communication. Speak from your heart and always be truthful and authentic in what you say. Prov. 25:11 says, "A word fitly spoken is like apples of gold in settings of silver." Always show respect when you speak with people. Treat others as you would like to be treated. They'll listen to you more when they feel you genuinely care about them. You're here to help make the lives of other people better. Add value to the words you speak. Show them how what you're saying can be a great benefit to their lives.

What you say effectively can change anything. John Maxwell said, "Effective communication is all about serving your audience through values-based influence." When you speak, keep it simple and direct. Don't make things complicated. Say what you have to say in a way that your audience can receive and understand it clearly. God calls us to share His truth, but the way we communicate is just as important as the message itself. Scripture tells us that a word fitly spoken is like apples of gold in settings of silver (Proverbs 25:11). This reminds us that how we say something can make the difference between hearts being opened or closed. When you speak, consider the ears and hearts before you. Are your words heavy with judgment, or gentle with understanding? Are they confusing, or do they illuminate the truth simply and clearly? God honors honesty, but He also honors wisdom. Speaking in a way your audience can receive is an act of love. It meets them where they are, not where you wish them to be.

Good communication is as much about listening as it is about talking. Men who are great know when to speak and when to have sacred silence. True communication is not measured by the words you speak, but by the hearts you touch and the ears you lend. Men of God understand that wisdom often comes in the pauses, in the sacred silence between words. Speaking without listening is empty; listening without understanding is fruitless. The greatest men know when to offer guidance, encouragement, or correction and when to simply be present, holding space for truth to reveal itself. Silence is not weakness; it is a divine pause, a place where the Spirit whispers, hearts are heard, and insight grows. To listen deeply is to honor God and others. Let your words be few but let your presence speak volumes. You get nowhere in a conversation if both people are speaking at once. You can't help others unless you learn to listen to their needs and desires.

James 1:19 says, "Let everyone be quick to listen, slow to speak, and slow to become angry." The Message Bible says, "Lead with your ears, follow up with your tongue." You must be willing to keep quiet and listen intently as others are speaking. If you struggle with this then pray and ask God to give you a listening heart. Take note that this is not a suggestion but a command. James is commanding all men to make it a habitual practice to listen more and speak less. Jesus said in Luke 8:18, "So take care how you listen." Good listeners make good friends. They make good learners, good teachers, and good counselors. To be a good communicator you must be a good listener so people will speak to you while at the same time be a good speaker so people will listen to you. To be a good listener you must look at the person you're talking to with eyes of love. Your eyes are the window to your soul, and they are a powerful tool for showing love to others. People can tell if you love them or not by the way you look at them.

One day a rich young ruler came to speak to Jesus and Mark 10:21 says, "Jesus felt genuine love for the man as He looked straight at him." He looked and He loved. Great communications start with the way you look at somebody. They've got to feel that you love them. They won't listen otherwise. Prov. 20:12 says, "God has given us eyes to see with and ears to listen with." Notice this verse doesn't say anything about the mouth. In a good conversation your eyes and ears matter more than your mouth. There is a reason God gave you two eyes and two ears and only one mouth. You should listen and look twice as much as you talk. The truth be told, the sound of silence is the best sound in any conversation. Why? Because the biggest need a hurting person has is to be listened to. Listen more and talk less. If you'll give people the freedom to speak, many times the solution will be revealed without you having to say a single word.

Since most problems are not solved overnight, it is imperative that you invest as much time as needed for the other person to say what's on their heart. To be a good listener you can't rush people along and push them to hurry up and get to the point. Great listening takes time so develop the gift of un-hurried listening. To truly listen is to honor the soul of an-other. In a world that moves fast, our hearts often keep pace with the clock instead of the person before us. But God teaches us through His Word that love is patient, and patience is the soil in which understanding grows. You cannot rush some-one's heart or mind. Great listening requires stillness, pres-ence, and the willingness to walk alongside another in their own time. When we slow down and give others the gift of our full attention, we mirror the way God listens to us - without hurry, without interruption, without judgment. In that sacred space of patience, hearts are opened, burdens are shared, and truth is revealed.

Great listening is an act of love, a reflection of God's patience, and a doorway to deeper connection. Consider Job 2:11-13, "When Job's three close friends heard of the tragedy Job had suffered, they got together and traveled from their homes to comfort and console him. Then they sat on the ground with Job silently for seven days and nights. And no one said a word, for they saw that his suffering was too great for words." This story teaches us that when you're dealing with somebody in pain, the deeper the sorrow, the fewer words you use. Just be-ing there for them is more than enough. Don't try to figure out what to say if someone is experiencing a personal crisis. Just show up and shut up. This is called the ministry of pres-ence. Rom. 12:15 says, "Weep with those who weep." There are few bonds like that of a common sorrow. When people are hurting, you're there to share their feelings. You must be willing to feel their pain before you try to find a solution to what they're going through.

Many times, we approach others with the desire to help - to fix, to solve, to offer solutions. Yet, the truth is, most people are not seeking a fix. What they truly long for is understanding, empathy, and a listening ear. God created us not only to act, but to bear one another's burdens in love. Sometimes, the greatest gift we can give is not advice or solutions, but our presence and our patience to hear their story, our compassion to sit with them in their struggle, and our silent prayers as they share their heart. Hurting people want to talk about their problems, and they want you to listen to them. Listening is an act of faith. It reflects God's love, who first listened to us, and who knows our struggles intimately. By simply being present, we honor their journey, and often, we allow God's wisdom to work in ways that rushing to "fix" never could. Remember, the Spirit sometimes moves not through words of correction, but through the quiet power of understanding hearts.

People will not care what you know until they know that you care. If the solution to their problem is the only thing on your mind, that's a sign you're not listening. Prov. 18:13 says, "Anyone who answers quickly without listening first is both foolish and insulting." This is another way of saying be quick to listen and slow to speak. Even if you know the solution, don't say what it is. Listen first. You need to feel what they're feeling before you try to fix anything. The solution can wait. Let people say what they feel they need to say. Listen to them and give them the freedom to unload what's weighing them down. Healing comes when you do this. Some people are not good at expressing themselves and how they feel but listening helps you tune in to the fear or hurt behind the words they're saying. Your ears are a healing tool used by God. If you'll learn to listen to people many of them will be healed right then and there simply because you kept quiet as they spoke.

You need to draw out of people what's really on their mind. When they're done talking say, "Tell me more." This allows them to dig deep into their soul to see what's there. Saying this shows love. It tells the person you're talking to that you're paying attention to them and that you really care what's going on in their life. It is also important that you be open-minded when you talk and listen to people. Never judge them or their situation until you have all the facts. This also will make you a great listener. Prov. 18:13,15 says, "What a shame - yes, how stupid! - to decide before knowing the facts! A person with understanding gets the facts and the wise person listens to learn more." Don't be presumptuous and don't think you know everything. Keep an open mind and don't make snap judgments. The more you listen, the more you'll learn what the facts are. Once you've listened, the time will come when God will have you speak to the individual. Good communication is not just listening, it's also speaking.

A good speaker not only knows what to say, they know when to say it. Timing is everything. Saying the right thing at the wrong time can bring very bad results. No matter how important the thing is you want to say, you must save it for the best time and place. The person you're talking to may not be receptive otherwise. The best time to say something is not when you're ready to say it, it's when the person is ready to receive it. Eccl. 3:7 says there is "a time to be silent, and a time to speak." Wisdom knows the difference. As you're waiting for the right time to come, you keep your ears open and your mouth shut. You can't speak the right thing at the wrong time. Eccl. 8:6 (MSG) says, "There's a right time and a right way for everything even though, unfortunately, we miss it for the most part." Don't just blurt out what you have to say when you want to say it. Be patient and the right time will come. As you wait, pray and plan what to say and how to say it.

Even Jesus did this. He said, "I have not spoken on My own power. Instead, the Father who sent me told Me what I should say and how I should say it" (John 12:49). Jesus was known for going off by Himself to pray. It was during these times when the Father would tell Him what to say and when and how He should say it. This is how you become a good communicator. If Jesus talked to the heavenly Father first, then you should also do the same. The bottom line is you must pray and plan. Never have a serious conversation when you're unprepared, when you haven't prayed and planned what to say. Prov. 16:23, "Intelligent people think before they speak." You must put your mind in gear before you put your mouth in motion. If you plan first, then what you say will be more persuasive. Smart people, men who are great, plan what to say ahead of time. Without proper preparation you would have no influence and no persuasion with other people.

Paul talked about planning in Col. 4:6 (GWT) when he said, "Everything you say should be kind and well thought out so that you know how to answer everyone." If you'll practice this one verse, if you'll be gracious in your speech and speak words with kindness, words that are well thought out, you will become a master communicator. Matt. 10:19,20, "Do not worry about what to say or how to say it. The right words will be there; the Spirit of your Father will supply the words." Your words will be better received if you let the Spirit of God speak through you. There will be no occasion to worry if you'll plan what to say and then pray about it. As you pray, ask God to help you to better understand what the other person is feeling, to see things from their point of view, to imagine yourself in their shoes. You'll know what to plan and pray for if you can understand their situation, their problems, when you see things from their perspective and feel their emotions.

In every conversation, the heart of true love is revealed not in what you say about yourself, but in how deeply you listen to and honor the needs of others. When you lay aside your personal desires and ambitions, you create space for genuine connection. You reflect the heart of Christ who came not to be served, but to serve. By giving prominence to the needs and desires of others, your words become vessels of encouragement, understanding, and grace. Silence your own agenda and speak life into the hearts of those around you. In doing so, you open the door for God's Spirit to work through you, transforming ordinary conversations into moments of divine impact. Remember: a conversation is not a stage for self-promotion, but a ministry of listening, validating, and uplifting.

When others feel heard, honored, and valued, you are not losing yourself but are walking in the fullness of God's love.

Eph. 4:29 (NIV) says, "Speak only what is helpful for building others up, according to their needs, that it may benefit those who listen." Let those you're speaking to start the conversation. Sit back and let them talk without interruption. Don't ask questions or for clarification. Just be quiet and let them speak. Take notes if questions come to you and ask them after they're done talking. This shows you care and you're paying attention to what they're saying. When they're done talking, summarize with them what you heard them say. Paraphrase it back to them to make sure you're both on the same page. When it's your time to speak, focus on the positive, not the negative. Speak favorably of what they can be doing and don't be critical of what they're not doing. Negativity don't change people. It puts them in a defensive mode to where they won't listen to what you have to say. Don't tell it like it is, tell it how it can be. Bring hope to people by painting a picture of a happy and bright future for them and their loved ones.

It is scientifically proven that what people focus on is what they move toward. Show them what they can become, don't tell them what they are. Be wise when you talk with people. Why? Prov. 15:2 (TEV) says, "When wise people speak, they make knowledge attractive." The Message Bible says, "Knowledge flows like spring water from the wise." It doesn't take any wisdom to share knowledge; it takes enormous wisdom to make it attractive. How do you make knowledge attractive? First, share the benefits. Be ready to tell people how what you're saying will be beneficial to them. Again, always speak in a positive manner. Prov. 16:21 (TEV) says, "A mature person is known for his understanding. The more pleasant his words, the more persuasive he is." A mature person does not just think deeply; he communicates thoughtfully. His words are seasoned with grace, kindness, and insight, making them not only pleasant to hear but also persuasive in guiding, encouraging, and influencing others.

Spiritually, this teaches us that God values how we speak as much as what we know. Knowledge alone can impress, but understanding, coupled with gentle and thoughtful words, builds bridges, heals wounds, and opens hearts. When your words are pleasant and grounded in understanding, they carry divine influence, reflecting the wisdom of God within you. You'll never be persuasive if you're abrasive. If you say something offensively, it will be received defensively. Being rude doesn't help anybody. Ask yourself: Are your words lifting others? Are they opening doors or closing them? Let your speech reflect the maturity God desires - words that enlighten, comfort, and lead others closer to His truth. When people are hurting, they need hope of a better future. Give it to them. Heb. 6:19 (NIV), "We have this hope as an anchor for the soul, firm and secure." If you offer people hope, they'll listen to you with open minds. Their walls will come down and you'll have an open door to speak life into their situation.

| 13 |

"WALKING IN FAITH"

To be great, you must be forever striving to please God. How do you do that? By walking in faith. Heb. 11:6 says, "Without faith it is impossible to please God." Faith is the key that unlocks the door of greatness for every man. Faith is the unseen confidence that God is who He says He is, and that He will do what He has promised. It is the courage to move forward when sight is limited and certainty is absent. Every man who has ever stepped into God-ordained greatness first learned how to walk by faith rather than by fear. Faith unlocks greatness because it aligns a man's heart with God's purpose. Without faith, a man remains trapped in the safe confines of logic and self-reliance. He may survive there, but he will never fully live. Faith dares him to step beyond what he can control and into what God has already prepared. When faith turns the key, the door opens to divine strength, wisdom, and authority that no human effort could produce.

Greatness is never revealed in comfort - it is revealed in obedience. Faith compels a man to obey God even when the cost is high and the outcome is unclear. It was faith that caused Abraham to leave familiarity, David to face Goliath, and Peter to step out of the boat. Each man discovered that on the other side of faith was not failure, but fulfillment. Faith also unlocks greatness by refining character. God is less interested in making a man impressive than He is in making him dependable. Through faith, a man learns patience in waiting, humility in success, and endurance in hardship. These qualities are the hinges upon which the door of greatness swings open. A man who trusts God in the unseen moments will be trusted by God in the visible ones. Most importantly, faith unlocks greatness because it connects a man to the power of God Himself. Greatness does not come from within us - it flows through us. Faith becomes the conduit through which heaven's resources meet earthly obedience.

Jesus said in Matt. 8:13, "Go your way; and as you have believed, so let it be done for you." Jesus is saying as you believe, you receive. Isn't that exciting? You can have anything you can imagine if you'll only believe. That's what faith is all about. The Bible says in Rom. 1;17 that those who have right standing with God will live by trusting in Him. In other words, greatness begins and ends with faith. It is not a hard thing to understand what faith is. Simply put, faith is seeing things from God's point of view. To walk in faith, you must see what God sees. Faith is not blindness; it is vision. It is the ability to look beyond what is visible to the natural eye and perceive reality through the eyes of God. Walking in faith is about seeing things in the realm of the spirit before they are seen with the natural eye. Heb. 11:1 (NLT) says we are "certain of things we do not yet see." Eph. 1:18 says, "I pray that the eyes of your hearts will be flooded with light so that you can see the wonderful future God has promised to those He called."

What is faith? It's the confident assurance that what you hope for is going to come to pass. You believe it is going to happen, you see it happening, and then it happens. Caleb had daring faith when he rose up and boldly said, "Let us go up at once and take possession, for we are well able to overcome it" (Num. 13:30). He had faith that he could have what God said he could have. He didn't let the presence of giants hinder him from claiming his God-given inheritance. Problems become smaller when you walk in faith. The size of your God determines the size of your problems. A big God equals small problems; a small God equals big problems. Like Caleb, men who are great have strong faith because they know and believe that nothing is too hard for the Lord, the God whose name is above every name. Luke 1:37 says, "For with God nothing will be impossible." Knowing this gives you the incentive to take risks, to get out of the boat when others don't.

Greatness comes by taking risks, by taking actions not based on how things are but on how they could be. The truth is, there is no success without taking risks. It's faith that opens doors for miracles to come in. Faith moves mountains and every miracle came about because somebody had the courage to take a risk and believe. Jesus said in Mark 11:22-24, "Have faith in God! If you have faith in God and you don't doubt, you could tell this mountain to get up and jump into the sea, and it would obey you. Whatever you ask for in prayer will be yours, if you only have the faith." Every time you use and stretch your faith, miracles happen. Faith moves God to act on your behalf. Jesus said in Matt. 9:29, "According to your faith will it be done to you." You get to choose how much God will bless your life. He will move in your life when you humbly expect Him to. That's faith and it's your confident expectation that pleases God and moves His hand on your behalf.

Make God happy by letting Him bless you because of your faith. Ps. 35:27 says, "Let the Lord be magnified, who has pleasure in the prosperity of His servant." Stop limiting God. Launch out into the deep and use your faith. Believe God to do big things in your life, things bigger than you've ever experienced before (Eph. 3:20). Too often, we place limits on a limitless God. Not with our words alone, but with our expectations. We believe Him only as far as our comfort allows. We trust Him only where we can still see the shore. Yet God has never worked within the boundaries of human reasoning - He works beyond them. When Jesus told Peter, "Launch out into the deep" (Luke 5:4), He was calling him away from disappointment, exhaustion, and shallow thinking. Peter had already tried and failed. His experience said, "Nothing will change." But faith said, "At Your word, I will let down the net." The miracle didn't happen in the shallow water - it happened in the deep.

Shallow faith produces shallow results. As long as you remain where it feels safe, familiar, and controllable, you will only experience what you can manage on your own. But the deep is where human ability ends and divine power begins. The deep is uncomfortable, unseen, and risky but it is also where abundance waits. Stop limiting God by past failures. Stop limiting Him by present resources. Stop limiting Him by what seems reasonable. Faith is not agreeing with what you see; it is aligning with what God has said. When you dare to trust Him beyond logic, beyond fear, beyond your own strength, heaven responds. Launching into the deep means praying bigger prayers, obeying even when it doesn't make sense, and believing God for more than survival. It means believing Him for overflow. It means trusting that the same God who called you forward will sustain you there. The breakthrough you seek is not behind you, and it is not beside you - it is ahead of you, in the deep.

Faith always says "amen" which means 'so be it.' Say what Mary said to the angel Gabriel, "Let it be to me according to your word" (Luke 1:38). 2 Cor. 1:20 (TPT) says, "For all God's promises find their 'yes' of fulfillment in Him. And as His 'yes' and our 'amen' ascend to God, we bring Him glory!" Living a good life is a hard thing to do but faith gives you the power to hold on in tough times. It sustains you as it unlocks the promises of God. Men who are great understand that faith doesn't always take you out of the problem, it sustains you and takes you through the problem. David understood this when he said, "Yea, though I walk through the valley of the shadow of death, I will fear no evil for You are with me" (Ps. 23:4). Faith doesn't always calm the storm, but it does calm you in the storm. It causes you to sleep peacefully like Jesus did as the storm raged around Him. Faith gives the ability to bounce back when hard times come. Life isn't easy but with faith you get stronger and more resilient.

When you dare to believe, you'll learn God's purpose for your life. Eph. 1:11 (MSG) says, "It is in Christ that we find out who we are and what we are living for." You were created with a destiny to fulfill and by faith you'll learn what your heavenly assignment is. You'll also receive God's strength for daily living. Is. 40:29 (NLT) says, "God gives power to those who are tired and worn out, and He offers strength to the weak." It is faith that connects you to the power of God. Eph. 1:19 (TLB), "I pray that you will begin to understand how incredibly great His power is to help those who believe Him." What's more, vs.20 says, "It is the same mighty power that raised Christ from the dead." The same power that birthed the New Testament is at your disposal. God's power is supernatural and by faith it's all yours. Paul said in Phil. 4:13 (TEV), "I have the strength to face all conditions by the power that Christ gives me." AMP, "I am ready for anything and equal to anything through Him who infuses inner strength into me."

We are commanded to be great and to live victoriously in this world. This happens when by faith God's power and glory is manifested in us and through us. There is no limit to what you can do in God's kingdom here on the earth when your faith is alive and active. Miracles happen when you dare to believe. Charles Spurgeon said, "We know not how much capacity for usefulness there may be in us. But when Christ by His Spirit grips you, what can you not do?" Everything God does in your life is because of His grace and mercy and because of your faith. For this reason you should be forever striving to grow in your faith. Col. 2:7 (NLT) says, "Let your roots grow down into Him and draw up nourishment from Him, so that you will grow in faith, strong and vigorous." Genuine faith that is real and legitimate has the power to change your life, the power to answer your prayers, the power to make you great. The more you grow in faith, the more blessings you will have and the greater you will become.

Jesus said, "According to your faith will it be done to you" (Matt. 9:29). In other words, you get to choose if you'll fulfill your destiny and how great you will become. The good news is that faith works even when life doesn't. You need to understand that real faith is more than useless words you utter from time to time and weak-kneed prayers you memorized and recited as a child growing up. James 2:14 says, "Dear brothers and sisters, what's the use of saying you have faith if you don't prove it by your actions? That kind of faith can't save anyone!" Many people think they have faith when in fact they don't. They sound like they're saved but their lifestyle and actions don't back up what they say. Real faith is more than words. Jesus said in Matt. 7:21, "Not everyone who says that I am their Lord is going to enter the kingdom of heaven. The only people who will enter heaven are those who do what My Father in heaven wants them to do." It's not what you say that counts, it's what you do.

Faith is based on your actions, not the words you say or how you feel. Being emotionally moved and having goosebumps does not mean you're walking in faith. Being sympathetic toward someone who is hurting means nothing if you don't do something to help them (James 2:15-17). Faith not accompanied by actions is dead and useless. You'll do more harm than good to a hurting person if all you do is say, "Don't worry, be happy" or if you walk away promising to pray for them. These people don't need your words and prayers; they need your help. You can say a lot of words but it's not faith unless you do something about the problem they have. Real faith is practical. It gets involved with the needs of people. Real faith is not confined to words, feelings, or Sunday moments - it moves its hands and feet into the everyday needs of people. Faith that lives only in belief but never in action is incomplete. When people know you truly care, they'll open their heart to you so you can talk to them about Jesus.

Faith is more than the words you say and the emotions you feel. Also, real faith is more than an idea you debate. Some people would rather debate theology than practice it. For some people, faith is just an intellectual game. It's a mental challenge, a theology to be studied, a doctrine to be debated, an idea to be discussed. For these people, faith is nothing more than a conversation. They love to talk, talk, talk. They'll talk all day about God and faith. For them, it's all about talking and not about action. They would rather discuss the Bible than do what it says. They talk the talk but don't walk the walk. James 2:18 says, "I can show you my faith by the good things I do!" James is saying real faith is expressed in visible ways. You can see it by the works you do. Practical faith notices the hurting before it debates theology. It sees hunger and provides food. It sees loneliness and offers presence. It sees brokenness and responds with compassion. If someone tells you they're walking in faith, say to them, "Show me!"

1 Cor. 16:13,14 tells you what to do if you want to be great. It says, "Stand firm in the faith. Stay brave, be strong, and do everything in love." Real faith always produces a changed life. When God comes into your life, it is impossible for you to not be changed in a positive and visible way. Faith is more than saying you believe in God. After all, even the devil and his demons do that. They believe in God but you won't find them in heaven. For sure, the devil is no atheist. It's one thing to have head knowledge about God, it's another thing to obey God, to love Him, trust Him, and serve Him. Faith without works is dead. You must act on what you say you believe. James 2:20, "It's foolish to not realize that faith in God is useless if you don't do what He wants you to do." Real faith is something you do. It's active and not passive. It's a commitment to obey God at all costs. Choosing faith is choosing God's will above your own, day after day. It is a conscious decision to align your life with His purpose.

True faith begins where comfort ends. It is the deliberate choice to obey God, not only when His will aligns with your desires, but especially when it challenges them. Faith says, "Not my will, but Yours be done," even when the cost is high and the outcome is uncertain. To walk by faith is to surrender the right to be in control. It means trusting that God's wisdom is greater than your understanding and that His ways, though sometimes painful or confusing, are always righteous and good. Faith does not wait for all the answers before it obeys; it moves forward because it knows who God is, not because it knows what will happen. Obedience at all costs is the proving ground of faith. Anyone can trust God when the path is easy, but faith is revealed when obedience requires sacrifice - when it demands letting go of personal ambition, comfort, reputation, or security. In those moments, faith declares that God is worthy of absolute allegiance, even when obedience feels costly.

The story of Rahab teaches us that your faith is more important than your background. 2 Cor. 5:17 says, "Old things have passed away; behold, all things have become new." Rahab was a prostitute who lived in the walled city of Jericho. She was not a Jew but because of her faith God used her in a mighty way. Joshua sent spies into Jericho and when the authorities found out they were there, Rahab hid them and risked her life to save them. James 2:25 says this was a work of faith for which she was greatly rewarded. Her and her family did not perish with those in the city who did not believe (Heb. 11:31). What's more, because she risked her life in order to save God's people, God put her in the genealogy of Jesus (Matt. 1:5). It matters not what your background is. Rahab was a harlot but she had faith and God said, "That's good enough for Me." By hiding the spies she was putting action to her faith. Her faith was demonstrated by what she did. She made no faith confessions but let her actions speak for her.

We learn from Rahab that our behavior shows what we really believe. We can all talk the talk but how many of us walk the walk? Are you great? Are you walking in faith? There's one way to find out. 2 Cor. 13:5 says, "Examine yourselves to see whether you are in the faith; test yourselves." The Message Bible says, "Test yourselves to make sure you are solid in the faith. Don't drift along taking everything for granted. Give yourself regular checkups." Testing yourself in the faith is not about questioning whether God is faithful; it is about honestly assessing whether your life is aligned with what you confess. Faith is more than words spoken on Sunday - it is the daily posture of the heart, revealed through obedience, humility, endurance, and love. God is calling you to daily examine the quality of your walk with Him. The greatness of a man of faith is evidenced by an obedient walk with Christ. Look in the mirror and examine yourself honestly to see if you are living a dynamic, faith-oriented life.

Charles Spurgeon said, "Go right through yourselves from the beginning to the end. Stand not only on the mountain of your public character but go into the deep valley of your private life. Look not only at your performance, which is but the product of the soil, but dig into your heart and examine the vital principle." Men who are great have a character that is dependable. When you are dependable you are loyal, you keep your word, and you stay true to biblical standards. Men who are dependable exercise care, persistence, and determination in ensuring excellence in what they do. They do their best by paying attention to detail. Being great makes you a man with high standards. You refuse to live beneath the level God designed for you. You go above and beyond what normal people reach for. For you, being good is not good enough. Greatness is second nature to you. It flows out of you wherever you go. The world is a better place because you and your greatness are in it.

| 14 |

"LEAPING FORWARD"

All men are called to be great in a world that is literally falling apart. Every day some crisis or another is reported on the evening news. To be great you must develop mental toughness and have strength of character. You must be flexible and be able to adapt to the continual stresses of life, to unexpected turns, changing seasons, and unplanned burdens. Greatness is not forged in moments of ease, but in the quiet, unseen battles of the mind and heart. You need the kind of inner strength that stands firm when circumstances shake you, when pressure presses in, and when the path forward is unclear. Mental toughness is the discipline to guard your thoughts, to refuse despair, and to choose faith over fear even when the storm does not immediately pass. Strength of character is the backbone of a great life. It is built when convictions are held without compromise and integrity is maintained when no one is watching. Character is proven not by how loudly one speaks, but by how faithfully one lives.

Every challenge, every delay, and every disappointment becomes a refining fire, shaping a heart that is steadfast, humble, and true. Yet greatness also requires flexibility. The rigid break under pressure, but the spiritually strong learn to bend without losing their foundation. Those who endure are those who adapt without abandoning their purpose. Flexibility is not weakness; it is wisdom. It is the ability to adjust your methods while remaining anchored to your calling. Spiritually mature people understand that pressure is not sent to destroy them, but to develop them. Like a tree whose roots grow deeper in the wind, adversity drives you into deeper dependence on God. Each stress becomes an invitation to grow stronger, wiser, and more resilient. True greatness is the harmony of toughness and tenderness, conviction and adaptability. It is the soul that refuses to quit, the mind that remains disciplined, and the heart that stays open to God's shaping hand.

When you develop mental toughness, cultivate strength of character, and learn to adapt through life's continual stresses, you discover that greatness is not something you achieve - it is something you become. In ancient China the symbol for "crisis" is the same as the symbol for "opportunity." A Chinese proverb says, "Crisis is an opportunity riding the dangerous wind." Denis Waitley once said, "The best way to adapt to change and lead a successful life is to view crisis as opportunities and stumbling blocks in your path as stepping-stones to the stars." Men who are great have the ability to adapt to life's challenges. This gives them immunity against anxiety and all the adverse responses to stress. Nelson Mandela once said, "Do not judge me by my success, judge me by how many times I fell down and got back up." A real man is resilient. He's able to adapt to stressful life changes and bounce back from hardship. He moves on despite the difficulty and grows from it.

The Bible contains many admonitions to press on (Phil. 3:13,14), to overcome hardship and temptation (Rom. 12:21), and to persevere in the face of trials (James 1:12). Paul said, "We are hard pressed on every side but not crushed; perplexed but not in despair; persecuted but not abandoned; struck down but not destroyed" (2 Cor. 4:8,9). Great men know on the other side of a trial is the strength to overcome it. J. K. Rowling said, "Rock bottom became the solid foundation on which I rebuilt my life." Resilience is not just bouncing back, it's leaping forward. It's your consistent resistance to never give up, to never let the trials of life take you down. President Woodrow Wilson said, "The difference between a strong man and a weak one is that the former does not give up after a defeat." We all have battles to fight and it's in these battles what men become great. Failure will never overtake you if your determination to succeed is strong enough.

To key to being an overcomer is to look to Jesus as our model for enduring tough times. We're to follow His example of resilience and stress management. Heb. 12:1,2 says, "And let us run with endurance the race God has set before us. We do this by keeping our eyes on Jesus, on whom our faith depends from start to finish." Jesus was very resilient. Vs. 3 says, "Think about all He endured when sinful people did such terrible things to Him, so that you don't become weary and give up!" Nobody experienced greater stress than Jesus. He was under enormous pressure. He was criticized often and misunderstood. There were constant demands on His life. He had little privacy and people were constantly trying to kill Him. That's stress but through it all He walked and lived with amazing peacefulness. No matter how difficult the situation became, He had a calmness and a resilience in the face of all the outrageous demands that were put upon Him.

To be the same way, to be great, you must keep our eyes on Jesus. You must follow His example of endurance and learn His secrets of resilience. When under stress, Jesus always remembered how much the Father loved Him. The principle of compassion is the first antidote to stress. Jesus talked about the Father's love over and over again. He said in John 10:17, "The Father loves Me because I sacrifice My life so I may take it again." Knowing and remembering that God loves you unconditionally, continuously, and extravagantly is the foundation of a resilient life. Stress flees when you know God is on your side. You are no longer facing life from a position of vulnerability, but from a place of divine backing. Paul knew this to be true when he asked the question, "If God be for us, who can be against us?" (Rom. 8:31). When captured by the enemy David wrote, "In God, whose word I praise, in God I have put my trust; I shall not be afraid. What can mere man do to me?" (Ps. 56:4).

Never doubt God's love for you. 1 John 3:1, "How great is the love the Father has lavished on us, that we should be called children of God! And that is what we are!" The Passion Translation says, "Look with wonder at the depth of the Father's marvelous love that He has lavished on us! He has called us and made us His very own beloved children." Men who are great know that the Father loves them as much as He loves Jesus (John 17:23). For this reason, they always get back up when the world knocks them down. The strength of a man is not found in pretending he never hurts, but in trusting God enough to stand again while still aching. Each time he rises, his faith grows stronger, his character deeper, and his dependence on God more complete. What once knocked him down becomes the very thing God uses to build him. Nobody said it better than David in Ps. 23:4, "Yea, though I walk through the valley of the shadow of death, I will fear no evil for You are with me."

In the midst of stressful trials, you must always remember who you are in Christ. Without the principle of identification you'll be overcome by the pressures of life. Not knowing who you are makes you more prone to stress. You'll be whipped around and manipulated and molded by problems and those around you. The world doesn't like people who are different than they are. If you don't walk in greatness, if you don't know who you are, the world will try to fit you into its mold. Be like Jesus who never had any doubts about His identity. He knew exactly who He was. Eighteen times in scripture He publicly defined Himself. For example, He said "I am the bread of life" (John 6:35), "I am the light of the world" (John 8:12), "I am the door" (John 10:7), "I am the good shepherd" (John 10:11). Over and over again Jesus said who He was. "I am the resurrection and the life" (John 11:25), "I am the way, the truth, and the life" (John 14:6), "I am the true vine" (John 15:1).

Jesus didn't need other people telling Him who He was. He said in John 8:18, "I testify on My own behalf." He didn't depend on the opinions of others to validate Himself. When you're great it doesn't matter who other people say you are. Too often, we allow the opinions of others to shape how we see ourselves. People will doubt you, criticize you, and even try to define you by their own limitations. But true greatness is not determined by human approval - it is measured by the purpose God has placed within you. Never depend on the opinions of others. If you do, you'll be prone to stress. Instead, be the man God created you to be. Jesus said, "You are the salt of the earth. And you are the light of the world. Don't hide your light" (Matt. 5:13-16). Step into your calling. Embrace the gifts God has placed in you. Walk boldly in the path He has set before you. The problem is, if you don't know who you are, other people will decide for you. They'll force you into their mold and they'll create stress in your life.

You will become resilient in overcoming when you're fully convinced who it is you're trying to please in your journey through life. The principle of motivation helps you know who you're living for. What is it that motivates you every day? If you don't know, you will be prone to come under stress. Jesus said, "No one can serve two masters. Either you will hate the one and love the other, or you will be devoted to the one and despise the other" (Matt. 6:24). Let's face it, you can't please everybody. Trying to brings enormous amounts of stress. Even God can't please everybody. One person prays for rain while another prays for sunshine. Prov. 29:25, "The fear of man brings a snare, but whoever trusts in the Lord shall be safe."

The Message Bible says, "The fear of human opinion disables, trusting in God protects you from that." Men who are great live to please God wholeheartedly. Jesus said in John 5:30, "I am not trying to do what I want, but only what My Father who sent Me wants."

True greatness is not measured by wealth, fame, or the praise of men. The mark of a man who is truly great in God's eyes is a heart fully devoted to Him. Such a man seeks first to honor God in every decision, every action, and every word. His greatest desire is to walk faithfully in God's will, to serve others in love, and to reflect the character of Christ in all he does. Jesus was resilient over stress because He was only trying to please one person. He said in John 8:29, "I always do those things that are pleasing to Him." Pleasing God will simplify your life because you no longer worry if you're pleasing everybody else. Jesus never let approval or rejection control Him and neither should you. Paul said in Gal. 1:10, "I'm not trying to be a people pleaser! No, I am only trying to please God. If I were still trying to please people, I wouldn't be Christ's servant." You can't please everybody so don't try. Please God only and your resilience over stress will flourish.

Another key to being resilient and overcoming stress is to know your calling. You must know beyond a shadow of a doubt what God has called you to do with your life. If you don't know what your calling is, the principle of vocation will compel you to spend time alone with God until you know that you know what your heavenly assignment is. This is so important because if you don't know why you're here you'll be more prone to stress. You won't know if you're coming or going. Be like Jesus who knew exactly what He was called to do. He said in John 8:14, "I know where I came from and I know where I'm going." Jesus lived a purpose driven life, and you are called to do the same. The word "drive" means 'to guide, to control, to direct.' Great men are driven by their God-given purpose, by a divine assignment planted in their hearts by God Himself. Every step they take, every decision they make, is fueled by a vision that transcends personal gain. They are driven by a calling greater than themselves.

A man aligned with God's purpose walks with unwavering determination, knowing that setbacks are not roadblocks but refining moments. His life becomes a beacon, inspiring others to seek their own God-given destiny. When purpose leads, power follows; when God directs, greatness endures. Remember that the measure of a man is not in what he acquires, but in how fully he lives out the mission God placed within him. Knowing your purpose is paramount because it helps you determine what's important and what's not. Knowing the direction your life is supposed to take eliminates stress. Until you know what your calling is, you are more likely to be controlled by others. They'll tell you what to do when you should be letting God tell you what to do. Everybody, it seems, has a plan for your life. If you listen to them doubt will roll in like a tsunami wave bringing with it stress and despair. Waste no time in finding out what your calling is and then go out and do what God has called you to do.

162 - RANDALL J. BREWER

Make no mistake about it, the devil will try to distract you from fulfilling your heavenly call. This is why you must always focus on what matters most. The principle of concentration prevents you from being distracted by less important things. Being great is a matter of priorities, of putting God's will above your own. Jesus was a master of concentration. He focused His life like a laser, and He refused to be distracted from what the Father called Him to do. An example of this is found in Luke 9:51, "As the time drew near for His return to heaven, He moved steadily onward toward Jerusalem with an iron will." He had a goal for He knew what His calling was and He always clarified what His priorities were. On His way to the cross He was persistent, determined, and focused. Paul was the same way. He said, "This one thing I do" (Phil. 3:13). These words reveal the heart of a man fully focused on his spiritual calling. Single-minded focus is the name of the game. It's how your potential comes to full fruition.

To be great you must be a man of single purpose with one aim and one ambition. You must be like an Olympic runner who has but one goal after the gun goes off. God does not multiply your fruitfulness by dividing your attention; He multiplies it when you dedicate yourself fully to His calling. Single-minded focus requires discipline, prayer, and sometimes the courage to say "no" to good things in order to say "yes" to God's purpose for your life. When your heart, mind, and efforts are aligned toward God's vision for you, what once seemed impossible begins to manifest. Your talents sharpen, your opportunities align, and doors open that only God could orchestrate. Go to war against distractions with fierce fighting and deep concentration. Be determined to obey God. Let "this one thing I do" become a reality in your life. Minister Alexander Maclaren said, "What a noble thing any life becomes that has driven through it the strength of a uniting single purpose."

To be resilient to the pressures of life it is vitally important that you spend quality time alone with God. It is imperative that you do this. Indeed, it is absolutely essential that you daily spend time alone with God for it will build within you a resilient spirit that will help you manage chronic stress. Prayer and daily fellowship with God is a great stress reliever. It's through the principle of meditation that you're able to cast all your cares upon the Lord (1 Peter 5:7). Jesus knew how important this is. Luke 22:39, "It was Jesus' habit to go out to the Mount of Olives to pray, and His disciples followed Him." A habit is something you develop through practice and reputation. It's when you do something over and over again. When you do something often enough, it becomes second nature to you. Jesus put forth much effort to do this. He would leave the city of Jerusalem, go across the valley to the Mount of Olives and pray there. You need to follow His example because you need quiet times to renew, to reflect, to recharge.

You were never meant to face life alone so the final key to being resilient is to get involved in a small group for moral and spiritual support. From the very beginning, God designed humanity for connection, for fellowship, and for mutual encouragement. Life's challenges with all its trials, disappointments, and seasons of uncertainty can feel overwhelming when shouldered alone. But God never intended for you to bear these burdens in isolation. Joining a small group of believers provides more than just company - it provides moral support, spiritual guidance, and the accountability needed to grow in faith. In the presence of others, your struggles are shared, your victories are celebrated, and your spirit is strengthened. Eccl. 4:9-10 reminds us that "Two are better than one. If either of them falls down, one can help the other up." When we walk together in fellowship with other men we have someone to lift us when we stumble, to encourage us when we feel weak, and to celebrate with us in moments of victory.

When Jesus began His ministry, the very first thing He did was gather a small group of men - His disciples. This wasn't a coincidence. Jesus understood the journey of life, especially the journey of faith, is not meant to be walked alone. He knew the power of fellowship, accountability, and shared purpose. In forming His small group, Jesus created a circle of influence, learning, and spiritual growth. Each disciple learned from Him, but they also learned from one another. They encouraged, corrected, and carried each other's burdens. Together, they became stronger, more effective, and prepared for the work God had called them to do. There is a vital lesson to be learned here. God often calls us to walk in purpose, but He doesn't intend for us to walk in isolation. Surround yourself with a small, faithful group of men because great things happen in the fellowship of the faithful, and just as Jesus demonstrated, small groups can become the launching pad for extraordinary kingdom impact.

| 15 |

"EMBRACE CHANGE"

Change happens to everybody. Sometimes those changes are good, other times not so good. To be great you must be able to adapt to the changes that come your way. To change means to go in another direction. The Bible says in Prov. 16:9 says, "A man's heart plans his way, but the Lord directs His steps." Greatness is not proven by how tightly you cling to what is familiar, but by how faithfully you respond when God allows change to enter your life. Change is not the enemy of purpose - it is often the instrument God uses to shape it. The seasons in which we walk are constantly shifting. Our anchor is unchanging, but our methods, expectations, and paths must often adjust. To be great in the eyes of God, you must learn to adapt without losing your identity. Trees that refuse to bend in strong winds are uprooted, but those that yield survive the storm and continue to grow. In the same way, spiritual maturity is revealed in your ability to yield to God's leading when circumstances change.

Adaptation is not compromise; it is cooperation with divine wisdom. God often uses change to stretch your faith. What once worked may no longer work, not because God has failed, but because He is calling you higher. Israel had to leave Egypt, Abraham had to leave his homeland, and the disciples had to leave their nets. Each transition felt uncertain, yet every step of obedience positioned them for greater purpose. God said in Is. 43:19, "See, I am doing a new thing! Now it springs forth; do you not perceive it?" The tragedy is not change itself but failing to discern God within it. When you adapt with faith, change becomes a classroom, not a crisis. You begin to see setbacks as setups, delays as development, and detours as divine direction. True greatness is forged in those moments when you refuse to grow bitter and instead choose to grow better. To be great you must embrace change with prayer, wisdom, and obedience. Hold tightly to God, but loosely to your plans.

Those who learn to adapt under God's hand discover that change does not diminish them - it prepares them. And in that preparation, true greatness is born. This is why you should embrace change when you know it comes from God. Is. 46:10 says He knows the end from the beginning and this is why you must forever submit to His divine direction. The Message Bible says in Job 25:2, "God is sovereign. He is awesome and everything in the cosmos fits and works in His plan." God is the master planner. He has planned everything in the universe and in history. He allows us to make decisions with the expectation that they will fit in with His plans. Consider Job 37:12, "The clouds turn around and around under His direction. They do whatever He commands throughout the earth. If clouds obey the plans of God, then you should also. Why? Ps. 33:11 (TEV) says, "God's plans endure forever; His purposes last eternally."

Our plans may last no longer than five minutes, but God's plans are set in stone. Is. 14:27 (NCV), "When the Lord all-powerful makes a plan, no one can stop it." This verse reminds us that God is not a hesitant planner nor a fragile dreamer. His purposes are not subject to human approval, political power, or spiritual opposition. When the Lord forms a plan, it is already infused with authority, wisdom, and inevitability. Many of our struggles come from living as though God's will is uncertain or easily overturned. We worry about resistance, delays, or enemies, forgetting that none of these can veto what God has determined. The hands of men may resist, circumstances may seem to contradict, and time itself may test our patience but none of these can cancel what God has ordained. This truth brings both comfort and correction. Comfort, because it assures us that God's promises over our lives are not hanging by a thread. Correction, because it calls us to stop fighting God's plan when it doesn't align with our own.

When God plans something, He sees the end from the beginning. He accounts for every obstacle before it ever appears. What looks like delay to us is often divine alignment. What feels like opposition is frequently the very proof that God's plan is advancing. If the Lord All-Powerful has made a plan concerning you, your family, your calling, or His kingdom, you can stand firm. No resistance is strong enough. No enemy is wise enough. No failure is final enough. What God has planned will stand because He stands behind it. So stop thinking the world will end if you don't get your way, if your plans don't come to pass the way you'd like them to. God is in control. There are battles that are lost and battles that are won but ultimately God will have the last word, and it is good. Whether you are celebrating a victory or enduring a setback, always remember that God reigns, God redeems, and God finishes what He starts. And when He speaks the final word over your life, it will be filled with grace and everlasting good.

God has His plans and they are eternal. Prov. 19:21 says, "People can make all kinds of plans, but only the Lord's plan will happen." Consider also Prov. 16:33 (CEV), "We make our own decisions, but the Lord alone decides what happens." The Message Bible says, "God has the final say." You may have your own plans for your life but God's plans are custom-made for you. So what should you do when God changes your plans? He's trying to get your attention so give it to Him. Some people are poor listeners. They're so busy talking they don't have time to listen to anybody, especially God. The problem many people have is they make their own plans without consulting God. This is why God said in Ps. 81:13 (NCV), "I wish My people would listen to Me." Many times, He has to change our plans because we're not listening to Him. If we were listening, we'd know what His will is and we would have gotten in with His plan.

James 4:13-15 talks about people who made their own plans. "Now listen, you who say, 'Tomorrow we will go to this or that city, spend a year there, carry on business and make money'" (vs. 13). These appear to be good plans but notice that God is not mentioned in these plans. They didn't consult God and listen to hear what He had to say regarding these plans. Vs. 14,15 then says, "Why, you do not even know what will happen tomorrow. Instead, you ought to say, 'If it is the Lord's will, we will live and do this or that.'" How do you find the Lord's will? You listen to Him. You bring God into your planning. If you'll do that, He won't have to change your plans as often as He does. God can see the future, you can't. He wants you to listen to Him to keep you from walking into dead ends, to spare you from problems you wouldn't normally have. Prov. 16:25 (NLT), "There is a path before each person that seems right, but it ends in death." What appears to be a good decision can turn out to be a disaster.

Listening to God is always for your benefit. The truth be told, you are limited in your perspective. You can't see the whole picture, but God can. He knows the pain that will result from a wrong decision. When God changes your plans it means He has a better plan. Jer. 29:11, "I have good plans for you, not plans to hurt you. I will give you hope for a good future." God's plan for your life is a good plan. If you understand that then you won't get upset when God changes your plans. You'll rejoice because He's looking out for you. Consider also that God's plan is more rewarding than your plan. Significance now and satisfaction here in this life comes from following God's plan and purpose for your life. These rewards also pass on into eternity. 1 Cor. 2:9, "No one has ever seen, heard, or even imagined what wonderful things God has ready for those who love

Him." You have no idea what God would like to do in you and through you if you would listen to Him and follow His plan.

The plan for your life is God's plan, but He lets you choose to follow it or not. He places it before you and then gives you the sacred gift of choice. You can walk in alignment with His will, or you can resist it. You can follow His voice, or you can follow your own. The choice is yours, but the plan remains His. When you choose God's way, you step into peace, even when the road is difficult. You discover meaning in the struggle and strength beyond your own. When you choose another path, God does not abandon you, but the journey becomes heavier, and the lessons more painful. God's plan is the highest plan, but obedience is the doorway into it. A lot of people miss God's plan for their life because they choose to go with their plan. They never say, "Thy will be done, not my will be done." We all have broken desires, but God's plan is bigger and better than you can ever imagine. People are not thinking big enough because they're not listening to God.

Every yes to God brings you closer to who you were created to be. Every step of faith opens doors that human effort cannot unlock. The question is not whether God has a plan for your life because He does. The question is whether you will trust Him enough to walk in it. It is not easy to experience a good life and to fulfill your heavenly call. Frankly speaking, God's plan for your life will be almost always harder than your plan. If you're looking for the easiest plan in life, don't ask God what His plan is. You'll learn quickly that God is more interested in your character than your comfort. God wants you to grow up and be great. He's not here to coddle you and His plan for your life can be difficult at times. It can bring confusion and pain. To be great you must have spiritual strength. God wants you to be a real man and not a wimp. He doesn't want you to be a baby that whines at everything. Whining keeps us focused on ourselves; maturity lifts our eyes to God's purposes.

We grow through pain. Pain is not God's absence; it is often His classroom. Growth rarely happens in comfort, because comfort asks nothing of us. Pain, however, demands a response. It presses us, stretches us, and exposes what is shallow so that what is strong can be built. Those who have suffered well carry a depth that cannot be learned any other way. They speak with authority not because they read the lesson, but because they lived it. If you are hurting, do not despise the process. God is not wasting your pain. He is shaping you, strengthening you, and preparing you for a greater purpose. Growth is rarely gentle, but it is always meaningful when placed in the hands of God. Men who are great endure much hardship in life because they're willing to put up with the pain in order to please their Heavenly Father and to receive their eternal reward. They know that whatever it is they're going through will eventually turn out for their good. It always does when you focus on God and not the problem.

It is God's plan that you trust Him and walk in faith during these hard times. This is why He doesn't explain everything to you in advance. Jesus told the twelve disciples in John 13:7, "You don't understand now what I am doing, but you will understand later." He's saying, "Trust Me in this." Why doesn't

God explain His plans to us in advance? Because He wants us to trust Him. He wants us to believe in faith the promise found in Rom. 8:28, "We know that all that happens to us is working for our good if we love God and are fitting into His plans" (TLB). Keep on trusting God when life doesn't make sense, when your plans get changed for one reason or another. Trust His wisdom and His timing and His love. Your faith gets tested every time your plans get changed. To pass the test all you have to do is trust God and all the promises He has given you. Know with certainty that God has a good plan and a good purpose for your life. Trust Him knowing that no weapon formed against you will prosper (Is. 54:17).

God will be with you no matter what happens. Trust Him wholeheartedly because cooperating with God's plan is the only rational way to live. Making plans for your life and the future is a good thing. After all, the Lord designed us with minds to think with and to make plans with. He also gave us a free will to make wise choices in life. One of the keys to greatness is to compare your plans with God's plan and will for your life. Put your plans in the hands of God and in His grace He will direct your steps. He'll guide you and bring you to the destination He desires you to go. Continue to make plans but have the faith to let God direct your steps. Ps. 138:8, "The Lord will work out His plan for my life, for His faithful love endures forever." Sometimes your plans are too small and too limited when compared to the big God we serve. Trust Him and He'll bring you to a place of rich fulfillment. Sometimes the plans you make are good and honorable but God may take you to a different destination with a different result.

When you walk by faith and trust His guidance, He will direct your steps and bring you to the place He wants you to be, a place He knows is best for you. You must be sure that whatever plans you make, the Lord will direct your steps and guide you in the right way you should go. Trust God because we all have a very limited view of the future. We don't know what will happen in the coming hours, days, weeks, months, and years. For safe keeping put your plans in the hands of God. Not only does He know the future, He holds the future in His hands. Take comfort knowing that while you have the freedom to make your plans, the Lord will step in and direct your steps in the way that is best for you. You need to thank God that He has given you the freedom to make future plans, for giving you the wisdom to make right choices in life. Along with those choices comes the wonderful assurance that God will direct your steps. He will guide you and give you all the wisdom you need.

Trust that God knows what He's doing as He strategically directs your steps. He's leading you on a path that will lead to blessings and favor. What do you do when your plan doesn't match God's plan. The answer is simple; you change your plan. You don't panic; you pray. You choose faith over fear. Don't be afraid to change your plans. 2 Tim. 1:7 (NCV) says, "God did not give us a spirit that makes us afraid but a spirit of power and love and self-control." Turn your thoughts to the wisdom and greatness of God. Don't worry but worship the King of kings and Lord of lords. Trust Him and He'll show you what His plan is. You don't decide what God's plan is for your life, you discover it. It's His plan that will give you the direction in life you must go. So what should you do? Get the plan. To fulfill your assignment, you must forever be ready for change. Be flexible and prepared to do what you've never done before and go to places you've never gone before.

Jesus told the rich young ruler to sell everything he had and come follow Him. The young man walked away sad because he had great riches. What was his problem? He wasn't ready and willing to change. Had he been willing to follow Jesus his life could have been the link in a long chain of miracles. God called Moses to change his plans at the burning bush. Moses wanted to remain a shepherd on the back side of the desert, but God had other plans. Moses was reluctant at first and tried to talk God out of sending him to Egypt to deliver God's people from slavery. But God had a plan and He was not to be denied. Moses eventually surrendered his will to God's will and the great exodus out of Egypt took place all because Moses was willing to change his plans. Changing your plans will not be hard if you have a holy reverence toward God, if you have a wholesome dread of displeasing Him. Never be afraid of people but always walk in the fear of the Lord.

Job 25:2 (CEV), "God is the one to fear because God is in control and rules the heavens." God is all powerful and His sovereignty is meant to bring you comfort. David understood this when he said in Ps. 23:4, "Your rod and Your staff, they comfort me." God will begin to direct your steps when you submit your will to His will. As He does this, you must be patient because it may take a little time to get you back on track. God said in Hab. 2:3 (TLB), "The thing I plan won't happen right away. Slowly, steadily, surely, the time approaches when the vision will be fulfilled. If it seems slow, do not despair, for these things will surely come to pass. Just be patient. They will not be overdue a single day." God's plan is a good plan and it's worth waiting for. James 1:4 says, "Let patience have its perfect work, that you may be perfect and complete, lacking nothing." You must learn to wait on God and give Him time to bring to pass the things He promised he would do. Truly this is one of the most powerful and beneficial things you can do.

In the Bible the word "wait" means 'to be in a position of readiness; to stay in a place of expectation; to look for watchfully." Why? Because good things are about to happen. Waiting on God paints a picture of a person sitting on the edge of their seat expecting something wonderful to happen at any moment. Waiting on God is fun and exciting. At least it's supposed to be. Always be joyful as you wait on God. It's what causes you to be strong and never give up. It gives God the freedom to do the work that needs to be done. Men who are great put their eyes on God and the plan He has for their life. Those who are great never worry because they know God is with them. Is. 43:2 says, "When you pass through the waters, I will be with you; And through the rivers, they shall not overflow you. When you walk through the fire, you shall not be burned, nor shall the flames scorch you." The Message Bible says, "When you're between a rock and a hard place, it won't be a dead end."

Believing that will put a smile of confidence on your face and the sound of joy in the words you speak. Those who walk by faith do so with great joy. There is joy in the journey because there is so much God has for you on the way to your destination. There's joy in believing He'll do what He says He will do. There is joy when you allow your imagination to soar above the clouds. Your faith is up there because you know God will do exceedingly, abundantly above all you could ask or think (Eph. 3:20). Being joyful is like reading the last chapter of a book before you read the first chapter. It allows you to see the glorious ending of your walk with God. You can have steadfast joy if you know the ending of the story, if you know that God is at work in the midst of your journey to please Him. God sees the end from the beginning, and you can too. At the end of your life you win, the devil loses, God is glorified. You can't have a better ending than that.

| 16 |

"THE WILL TO WIN"

Why were you born? You were born to be great. In order to be great, you must persevere during hard times, when the odds seem to be against you. The will to win is everything. Greatness is not born in moments of ease, applause, or certainty. It is forged in the unseen hours when the road is steep, the night is long, and the odds seem firmly set against you. It is in those seasons of pressure and resistance that the soul is tested and the true measure of faith is revealed. Hard times are not signs of abandonment; they are invitations to perseverance. The will to win is what carries you forward when strength feels scarce. It is the quiet decision to rise again, to keep believing, to keep pressing on when retreat would be easier. Scripture reminds us that endurance produces character, and character produces hope. Perseverance is the soil where greatness grows. Those who become great are not those who never struggle, but those who refuse to surrender their calling to discouragement.

When the odds are against you, remember that opposition does not determine your destiny - your perseverance does. Hold fast to the vision placed within you. Let faith fuel your determination. For the one who endures, who stands firm in the storm, who wills himself to continue when quitting whispers loudly, will ultimately discover that greatness was being formed all along. To persevere you will need a strong faith to stand on. This will allow you to bend without breaking, to grow when the winds of change blow your way. Being great causes you to look at the bright side of things even in the darkest moments of life. You just know that you know everything will be all right. To persevere means to look downstream for your gratification. You see the light at the end of the tunnel and all the rewards waiting for you there. It causes you to hope in a hopeless situation. That's what greatness is all about. It's knowing when the game of life ends you'll be declared the winner.

Believe God even when your circumstances are contrary to what He promises you can have. Believe God and be determined to never waver in your faith. If God said He would do something, then believe He'll do it. When you're convinced of that, you'll be great and you'll do great things. Regardless of any roadblocks or challenges, always maintain a resilient mindset and push through to the dream you are pursuing. Perseverance and determination keep you moving forward. It causes you to stay focused on the goal, to remain steadfast in your efforts to obtain victory and success. To be determined you've got to decide up front that you won't allow anything to make you quit. You've got to believe that no good thing will be withheld from you (Ps. 84:11). Perseverance is the battle you fight while you wait for the trial to end. It's the continual effort to do or achieve something despite difficulties, failure, or opposition. There is a blessing in persevering so stick it out and be determined to finish your race.

God will accelerate you because you're determined to give it everything you've got. When you're great God will put wind in your sails and give you the ability to do something you could never do on your own. 1 Cor. 16:13,14 says, "Be on your guard, stand firm in the faith, be courageous, be strong. Let everything you do be done in love." In life you're going to need faith, courage, and strength so be determined and stand firm. Resist the devil and he will flee from you (James 4:7). Always remember that faith doesn't make things easy, it makes things possible. Know also that nobody becomes great until they first overcome opposition. If you will endure hardness, you'll soon find that your suffering will eventually bring forth patience (James 1:3), joy (Ps. 30:5), knowledge (Ps. 94:12), and maturity (1 Peter 5:10). Suffering will refine your life and make you a better person (Ps. 66:10-12). It can be used to glorify God (John 9:1-3) and it helps make you more like Jesus (Phil. 3:10).

Men who are great know that the trials they go through causes godly character to be developed in their life. They know that no trial means no character. They also know that one of the worst things that can happen is for them to get delivered out of a trial God's using to build character in their life. A man who walks with God understands that trials are not punishments to be avoided, but tools in the hands of a loving Father designed to build something eternal within him. Hardships expose what is shallow and strengthen what is true. Pressure forges patience. Resistance produces endurance. Delay teaches trust. Every obstacle becomes a classroom where humility, obedience, courage, and perseverance are learned. What the enemy means for destruction, God uses for development. The fire that seems intended to consume is the very fire that purifies. Godly character is cultivated through surrender in the storm. Men who are great do not ask why trials come - they ask what God is forming through them.

Greatness in God's kingdom is not measured by how high a man climbs, but by how deeply he is formed along the way. This is why God never promotes men and make them great until they have first developed within themselves the character to succeed, when they persevere no matter what. Every man who has ever been born has been given a dream from God and a destiny to fulfill. Understand that the fulfillment of a heavenly call is not for the faint-hearted. There is an enemy out there who comes to steal, kill, and destroy (John 10:10). This means there will be obstacles you must face and tests you must pass before you fulfill your destiny. It takes greatness and strength of character to fulfill a heavenly call. If you want to succeed in life you must come up higher and obey God at all times. It is not hard to obey God if you trust Him and are daily walking in faith. You need to believe there are rewards if you obey God and serious consequences if you don't.

Your character effects your entire life. To ensure a long and successful life you need to obey God at all times and at all costs.

Obedience is one of the greatest character builders in the life of a believer because it reaches deeper than outward actions and touches the condition of the heart. It is easy to offer sacrifices like your time, your resources, even your talents while still reserving the right to do things your own way. But obedience requires surrender. It asks you to trust God's wisdom above your own understanding and to submit your will to His authority, even when the path is uncomfortable or unclear. The prophet Samuel captured this truth when he confronted King Saul and declared, "To obey is better than sacrifice"(1 Samuel 15:22). Saul had offered what appeared to be a religious act, but his disobedience revealed a heart that valued appearance over faithfulness. God was not impressed by the sacrifice because obedience is the true measure of devotion.

Obedience shapes character because it trains you to listen, to yield, and to walk humbly with God. Each act of obedience strengthens spiritual discipline, producing integrity, faithfulness, and perseverance. It teaches you to respond to God's voice promptly rather than selectively. Over time, obedience forms a life that reflects God's heart, not merely religious activity. Ultimately, obedience is an expression of love. Jesus Himself said, "If you love Me, keep My commandments" (John 14:15). Determine today to obey God at all times and leave the consequences to Him. He'll open doors you can't open and take you places you could never go on your own. Obedience may not always be easy, but you can do it when you realize that God is the sovereign ruler of the universe, and He knows what's best for your life. Setbacks will come but you must remain faithful at all costs. Press forward and give it everything you've got. Eccl. 9:10 says, "Whatever your hand finds to do, do it with all your might."

It is the responsibility of all men who want to be great "to contend earnestly for the faith which for once for all was delivered to the saints" (Jude 3). The Message Bible says you are to "fight with everything you have." Paul then tells us to stand up and "fight the good fight of faith" (1 Tim. 6:12). A "good fight" is a fight you win! 1 Cor. 15:57 says, "But thanks be to God who gives us the victory through our Lord Jesus Christ." Men who are great are not laid back and passive. They understand they have as much to do with the answer to their prayers as they expect God to be. There is a sign on the Colorado River that instructs whitewater rafters, "If you fall overboard you must be an active participant in your own rescue." For those who have the misfortune of falling into the swirling waters of the raging river, they must take charge of the situation they are in. They must actively participate in their own rescue and cannot lay back and let the rescuers do all the work. There is a part they have to play.

The same is true in the good fight of faith. For example, God gave the people of Israel the land of Canaan but wars had to be fought before they could possess it. Likewise, all men must press in to the things of God with a persistence and determination that will not rest satisfied until they receive what is promised. Jacob wrestled with God and said, "I will not let You go until You bless me" (Gen. 32:24-30). When Jacob grabbed onto God, he got grabbed by God and received his blessing. The only place where "success" comes before "work" is in the dictionary. Phil. 2:12 says to "work out your own salvation with fear and trembling." In order to live up to the full potential that your faith would allow you must pick up your sword and fight the good fight of faith. There is no other way. You were born to be great, and God is dishonored when you have a defeatist attitude. This is why you need to draw a line in the sand and tell the devil, "No more!" Proclaim out loud that no weapon formed against you will prosper.

David wrote in Ps. 34:19, "Many are the afflictions of the righteous, but the Lord delivers him out of them all." Victory is assured for men who are great. Rise up knowing you are equal to and ready for anything the enemy throws your way. That trial is no match for you so don't let it overwhelm you. Is. 51:9 says, "Awake, awake, put on strength, O arm of the Lord!" God has you in the palm of His hand and He's not about to let you go. There is anointed power in your life that protects you and enables you to overcome the wiles of the enemy. 1 John 4:4 says, "Greater is He who is in you, than he who is in the world." You need to realize that success is born out of adversity. Tests, trials, and failure come to all who believe. Matt. 5:45 says the rain falls on the just and the unjust. When trials do come, a decision must be made. Do roadblocks signal the end of your journey, or are they steppingstones to a better and abundant life? What seems like a setback may be a redirection toward a more abundant and purposeful life.

Paul asks, "If God be for us, who can be against us?" (Rom. 8:31). In Christ we always win if we don't run away and give up the fight. Men who are strong overcome the enemy. God said in Ps. 89:19, "I have given help to one who is mighty." The Message Bible says, "I've crowned a hero, I chose the best I could find." God chose you and this is why you are great. If a struggle comes your way, rise up above it knowing you and God are stronger than anything the devil throws at you. Men who are weak say "Woe is me!" when trials come their way but men who are great are different. They look the devil in the eye and say, "Bring it on!" Like a mighty eagle, you are called to rise above the storms of life. The Spirit of God lifts you, setting your heart and mind on higher ground, far above the turbulence of your trials. While others may be weighed down by fear, doubt, or difficulty, you glide effortlessly on the wind currents of God's presence, seeing your challenges from a divine perspective.

Eagles do not fight the wind - they use it to soar. Likewise, when you yield to the Spirit, what once threatened to hold you captive becomes the very force that propels you into victory. Your eyes, fixed on God, perceive hope where others see despair. Your soul finds freedom where others feel trapped. Rise, then, on the wings of faith. Live above the noise, above the fear, above the limitations of this world. Trust in the Spirit's power, for He carries you to heights you never imagined, and on those heights, your spirit soars unshaken, renewed, and victorious. Ps. 92:12 says, "The righteous shall flourish like a palm tree." During a hurricane a palm tree will bend over but it won't break. When the wind ceases to blow, the palm tree will bounce back to its original position. Its root system got stronger as it kept the tree from toppling over. Prov. 24:10 says a good man may fall seven times but each time will stand back up. There's the bounce back. This is when you flourish like a palm tree.

When the wind stops blowing, you'll still be standing strong. You'll be the head and not the tail, above and not beneath. You'll be the victor and not the victim. Now is the time to stretch your faith. If you stay in your comfort zone, you'll never see the power of God manifested that will take you into your personal Promised Land. God wants to do powerful things in your life, and you must be great for that to happen. God is mighty in strength and He wants to fill you with that same power. God is great (Job 36:26) and is exalted by His power (Job 36:22). This is the God who wants to enable you to carry out His will on the earth. He wants to make you great and powerful so He can do all the good pleasure of His will in you and through you. In other words, He wants to use you to change the world. James 4:14 (AMP) asks the question, "What is the nature of your life?" Why are you here? What is your life all about? An aching void will fill your heart if these questions are not answered.

An important truth in life is you only live once but, if you live a life rooted in love, guided by faith, and walking in integrity, once is enough. Living "rightly" does not mean a life free of mistakes, sorrow, or struggle. Rather, it is a life aligned with God's purposes, a life that seeks to love others deeply, forgive freely, and serve with humility. It is a life where every choice reflects your values and honors the divine calling within you. When you live in this way, each day becomes meaningful. Each encounter, each act of kindness, each moment of obedience adds to a legacy that transcends your years on earth. You do not need to live again, because a life lived rightly leaves no regrets, no unfinished business, no unanswered longing for what truly matters. Life is not measured by its length but by its depth. One life, lived with faith and love, is enough. Make every moment count. Walk in purpose. Love without hesitation. Serve without expectation. And let your life, once lived, shine as a testimony to God's glory.

You must take your mind off your problems and look at the big picture. You must rise up, cast all your cares on Jesus, and make your life count. Look beyond yourself and let your light shine in this dark world. Do you want to be great and fulfill your purpose in life? Then put God first in everything you do. Surrender yourself to the plan of God and you'll discover what greatness really is. Love God "with all your heart, with all your soul, and with all your mind" (Matt. 22:37). If you love Him, you'll obey Him no matter what He tells you to do. Being great means you'll do what God tells you to do, you'll say what He tells you to say, and you'll go where He tells you to go. Eph. 2:10 (MSG) says, "He creates each of us by Christ Jesus to join Him in the work He does, the good work He has gotten ready for us to do, work we had better be doing. God created you to do good works. The most exciting and fulfilling life you could ever have is to do what God created you to do.

God is building a kingdom in your midst and He wants you to be a part of it. 1 Peter 2:5 (NLT) says, "And you are living stones that God is building into His spiritual temple." The Message Bible says, "Present yourselves as building stones for the construction of a sanctuary vibrant with life in which you'll serve as high priests offering Christ-approved lives up to God." Jesus was born to serve (Phil. 2:7). He served the disciples by washing their feet. He served the hungry when He fed them. He served the sick when He healed them. He served the lonely and the outcasts when He interacted with and loved them. And He served you by dying on the cross for your sins. If Jesus served, so can you. Eph. 5:1,2 (NLT) says, "Imitate God in everything you do. Live a life filled with love, following the example of Christ." God has a plan for your life, and it matters not your age, gender, or nationality. There is something God wants you to do today, tomorrow, and the rest of your life.

Every day you need to have the desire to live at your full potential. Give God an open door into your life. Take your life and point it in the direction God wants you to go. You were made for greatness because you were created to do great things. You were chosen to show the world what God is like by the things you say and do. The world is made a better place when ordinary people respond to their heavenly call. This is what allows God to step in and do extraordinary things through them. Be great and let God use you. 1 Cor. 3:9 says, "For we are God's fellow workers." It is a great privilege to be regarded as laborers together with God. Other people need you and are counting on you. Pray daily and ask God to cause you to always be at the right place at the right time. The people of Ninevah needed Jonah and there are people who are counting on you to be the great person God called and created you to be. Placing a call on your life is God's part, answering the call is your part.

Daily keep your yourself in the will of God for this is what determines the direction your life will take. Each small step toward God's purpose is a victory, and every challenge overcome strengthens your testimony. Dedicate your life to Christ. Dedication is all about obedience. It's telling God you'll do whatever He tells you to do. It's saying, "Here I am! Send me" (Is. 6:8). Whatever you dedicate your life to is what determines the direction your life will go. If you'll do what God is telling you to do, you will see the fulfillment of your destiny. To be great you must be like Paul who said, "I press toward the goal for the prize of the upward call of God in Christ Jesus" (Phil. 3:14). The Message Bible says, "I'm off and running, and I'm not turning back." This is why he was able to say in 2 Tim. 4:7, "I have finished the race, I have kept the faith." Yes, Paul fought the good fight. In other words, he fulfilled his destiny. On the day you stand before Christ, hopefully you'll be able to say the same thing.

SUMMARY

From Genesis to Revelation, the story of Scripture is filled with ordinary men who stepped into extraordinary destinies - not because of their own strength, but because God appointed them, anointed them, and walked with them. Abraham, Moses, David, Joshua, Samuel, Paul, and countless others all shared one truth: they were born to be great because they were born to fulfill God's purpose on the earth.

Their greatness was not defined by fame, power, or earthly achievement, but by obedience, humility, and the courage to trust God in every season. Each man's life stands as a testimony of what God can do when someone yields fully to His call.

In the same way, every believer today carries the imprint of divine purpose. You, too, were crafted by God's hands, set apart for a destiny that only you can fulfill. The greatness God places within His people is not measured by human standards, but by the impact of a surrendered life - one that brings Him glory, advances His kingdom, and touches the lives of others.

As you close this book, remember this: Greatness is not something you chase - it is something you embrace. It is already within you because the God who created you designed you with intention, purpose, and destiny. Stand firm in your identity. Walk boldly in your calling. Live faithfully in the power of the Spirit.

You were born to be great and through Christ, you will do great things on the earth.

www.ingramcontent.com/pod-product-compliance
Lightning Source LLC
Chambersburg PA
CBHW070915130626
46555CB00001B/144

*9 7 9 8 9 9 4 1 2 2 3 4 1 *